Denise Buser

Unholy Discrimination

ReligionsRecht im Dialog

Law and Religion

herausgegeben von / edited by

Prof. Dr. Adrian Loretan
(Universität Luzern
University of Lucerne, Switzerland)

Band / Volume 25

LIT

Denise Buser

Unholy Discrimination

An overview of the legal rules governing
the consideration of the balance of interests between
gender equality and the freedom of religion
in access to leading spiritual offices

LIT

Printed with the support of the Berta Hess-Cohn Stiftung, Basel.

This book is printed on acid-free paper.

Bibliographic information published by the Deutsche Nationalbibliothek
The Deutsche Nationalbibliothek lists this publication in the Deutsche Nationalbibliografie; detailed bibliographic data are available on the Internet at http://dnb.d-nb.de.

ISBN 978-3-643-80245-3

A catalogue record for this book is available from the British Library

Klosbachstr. 107
CH-8032 Zürich
Tel. +41 (0) 44-251 75 05
E-Mail: zuerich@lit-verlag.ch http://www.lit-verlag.ch

Distribution:

In the UK: Global Book Marketing, e-mail: mo@centralbooks.com
In North America: International Specialized Book Services, e-mail: orders@isbs.com
In Germany: LIT Verlag Fresnostr. 2, D-48159 Münster
Tel. +49 (0) 2 51-620 32 22, Fax +49 (0) 2 51-922 60 99, e-mail: vertrieb@lit-verlag.de
In Austria: Medienlogistik Pichler-ÖBZ, e-mail: mlo@medien-logistik.at
e-books are available at www.litwebshop.de

Contents

Preface (to the German edition)

In summer 2002 seven women on a ship on the Danube were ordained priests *strictly in accordance with the Roman Catholic Rite of Ordination.* At the time the action attracted worldwide attention, but since then these female priests have dropped out of the news completely.

They have continued to work quietly and effectively. The most courageous among them agreed to be consecrated as bishops so that they could ordain more female priests.

In 2012 I decided to interview Dr Ida Raming, one of the seven ordained women. She agreed readily and a little while later in Stuttgart I was met by a tall, self-assured 80-year-old with a friendly smile – although she has sufficient reason to be bitter about her treatment as a theologian and intellectual: her public avowal of her priestly vocation was negated by the Vatican, a negation painfully reaffirmed several times, and her act of Christian conviction – ordination – was followed by excommunication.[1] Notwithstanding this, Ida Raming remains convinced that the ordination of women is a question of equality and justice – and, consequently, one of credibility as well.

The issue of *women's access to leading spiritual offices* is not limited to Catholic Christianity. This is the reason for three interviews. After the Catholic woman priest, two other women agreed to answer my questions: Bea Wyler, the only woman rabbi in Switzerland, and Rajaa Naji al Makkawi, a Moroccan law professor and authority on Islam.

The only stipulation was that the enquiry should focus on the legal issue. The starting point for all three interviews was the universality of the principle of gender equality and its relationship to the freedom of religion, which is similarly guaranteed as a fundamental right. The women, each an exponent of one of the world's three great monotheist religions, accepted this legal perspective, even though in principle one might well ask what the law has to do with religion (for an attempt to answer this see chapter one).

The focus of the following considerations is the legal conundrum of how to objectively evaluate the mutually exclusive positions of the principle of equality

---

1 The excommunication contained numerous defects under canon law; see chap. 5 and the references to the literature in *Demel* in fn. 176 and 183 below.

and freedom of religion as they pertain to women's access to leading spiritual offices and what conclusion can be drawn from this juxtaposition.

My view set forth in previous articles that the religious communities should pro-actively work to facilitate acceptance of justice in the gender question still holds. My aim in this paper is to show that an objective evaluation of the arguments and counterarguments underpins women's equality of access to leading spiritual offices. The starting point is the question of priesthood for women in the Roman Catholic Church. Whereas in other religions women are excluded from leading spiritual offices primarily on circumstantial grounds, in the Roman Catholic Church the question is more acute on account of a provision of the Code of Canon Law (CIC) (can. 1024 CIC: "Only a baptised male validly receives sacred ordination."). The exclusion of women from ordained ministry is a particularly striking example of an insurmountable obstacle to gender equality. That said, considerations about the question of priority between gender equality and freedom of religion are also applicable to other religious communities.

The title of this paper alludes to Gertrud Heinzelmann's *Die geheiligte Diskriminierung* (Sacred Discrimination), the lawyer's account of her famous petition of 23 May 1962 to the Second Vatican Council. It reflects the fact that the efforts of all protagonists – feminist theologians and lawyers and other women in solidarity with them – were important steps on the path to gender equality in the religious sphere.

I am deeply grateful to the following persons and institutions, without the valuable contributions of whom this study could not have appeared. I am indebted to Judith Stofer lic. theol. for her thorough copy-editing of the research and Monica Schwenk lic. phil. for proofreading the text.

My heartfelt thanks are due to my colleague and former teacher Professor Peter Albrecht for his critical review of the manuscript. It was a great pleasure to work with Professor Adrian Loretan. My decision to publish my volume in "ReligionsRecht im Dialog", the series that he edits, was influenced by his involvement in the discussion about gender in religion. I thank Ms. Isabel Opatz from the LIT-Verlag for her friendly and helpful support. I am much obliged to the Faculty of Law of the University of Basel for granting me a sabbatical during the 2013 spring semester, as it enabled me to devote my attention exclusively to exploring this topic.

Finally, I would like to express my sincere appreciation and thanks to the Freiwillige Akademische Gesellschaft Basel and the Berta Hess-Cohn Stiftung Basel, without whose generous support this study could not have been published.

Basel, November 2013
Denise Buser

Preface to the English edition

The translation of this book into English was made possible by the generous support of the Dialog zwischen Kirchen, Religionen und Kulturen Foundation and the Freiwillige Akademische Gesellschaft. The translation was done by BMP Translations AG in Basel. I am indebted to John Richardson and John Purnell for their careful work. The original German text has, where necessary, been updated.

Basel, October 2016
Denise Buser

Abstract

This study explores the conflict between gender equality and religious freedom as it pertains to the non-admission of women to leading spiritual offices. In the Roman Catholic Church, canon law excludes women from the priesthood (can. 1024 CIC "Only a baptised man validly receives sacred ordination."). Islam poses no comparable legal barriers, only social hindrances. In Judaism, too, de facto inequalities are the main hindrance to women's access to the rabbinate (apart from one inconsistently applied medieval provision). All of these processes are legally relevant forms of discrimination that violate natural and international gender equality law.

The contradiction between the fundamental right to non-discrimination and religious communities' appeal to their right to religious freedom must be resolved by evaluating the balance of competing interests. For the latter, arguments include the long-standing, unquestioned acceptance of tradition (argument of continuity), theological reasons ("God's eternal plan"), the danger of schism (as a result of opening up the priesthood to women) and stereotypical gender roles.

The arguments in favour of non-discrimination include, first, the specific features of equality conflicts in the religious field: the imbalance of power between the opponents, threats to leave the church (either-or problem) and the argument that an organization serves specific ideological or spiritual ends. Moreover, the fundamental rights of the adversely affected party must be given greater weight if the interfering party renders it completely impossible for the affected party to exercise its fundamental rights. In addition, the counterarguments must be taken into account in evaluating the competing interests of gender equality and religious freedom, for instance the weight of evidence of theological research supporting the ordination of women, the superseding of (tacit) consent to "the church of men" by more recent social dissent in this matter, and established practice in all religious communities (female parish administrators in the sanctuary in Roman Catholic churches, female rabbis in Liberal and Reformed Judaism, and female imams in mosques).

In this study the theoretical evaluation of the balance of interests is explored in practice in three specific case studies drawn from Roman Catholic Church practice (seminary access for a female theology student; equal payment for priests and female community administrators; and the voiding of the election of a female theologian ordained "contra legem"). The comparison and evaluation of the opposing positions on gender equality and religious freedom and the analysis of the arguments and counterarguments have led the author to conclude that the principle of gender equality should be valued more highly than the appeal to a long-standing tradition of male spiritual leadership that is widespread in all three major monotheistic religions.

Chapter 1 Introduction: Importance of the law for gender equality in religious communities and churches

Is the Roman Catholic Church practice of excluding women from ordination a discrimination that is relevant in law? Is there a gender-independent right to priesthood? Are there points of contact between the law and religion? In religion-related conflicts in fields subject to state regulation the state has to address the relationship between religion and statutory provisions. Three case studies serve to illustrate religious conflicts and conflicts of constitutional rights.

1.1. Negative formulation of exclusion

Two decades ago (1994), Pope John Paul II determined that priestly ordination is to be reserved to men alone in accordance with "God's eternal plan" and that "this judgement is to be definitively held" by all the faithful.[2] The papal declaration was intended to put an end to the on-going debate about the "women's issue" in the Roman Catholic Church in Catholic circles and academic theological publications. The definitive papal decision also answered in the negative the question of whether, given the undisputed fact of every religion's historical rootedness,[3] the exclusion of women from priestly ordination was not primarily a reflection of historical patriarchal circumstances. Citing the constant and universal tradition of the Church, the Apostolic Letter denies that the dimension of time in any way influences the question of admission to the spiritual ministry – and, hence, the possibility of adjusting to changing circumstances in society.

Taken to its logical conclusion, the assumption that the priestly ordination of women is excluded for all time is a disquieting one. If the priestly ordination is reserved to men alone, then, like the Roman Curia, one must conclude that the exclusion of women has *theological meaning*. The most obvious logical conclusion of this, in turn, is that the development of women's equality in the 21st century is, ultimately, not an expression of the will of God, at least not in the religious

2 Apostolic Letter Ordinatio Sacerdotalis (1994) of John Paul II to the Bishops of the Catholic Church (https://w2.vatican.va/content/john-paul-ii/en/apost_letters/1994/documents/hf_jp-ii_apl_19940522_ordinatio-sacerdotalis.html, accessed 7 October 2016).

3 See *von Arx*, p. 192.

sphere. Although this logical reasoning is not explicit in *Ordinatio Sacerdotalis*, it is implicit.

If the exclusion of women has theological meaning and, consequently, the involvement of women in the highest offices of a Church or religious community does not reflect God's will, the resulting situation is difficult to reconcile with the conception of man in modern societies based on the rule of law as found in those parts of the world with a Christian heritage. This gap between modernity and divinely transfigured misogyny is even less explicable given the Christian roots of the modern view of man. It cannot be denied that there is a *direct line* between fundamental Christian values such as charity and human dignity rooted in man's likeness to God and the modern view of man and woman in states that practise the rule of law.[4] As the modern state under the rule of law is a consequence of secularisation and the rise of the national state,[5] there was no need for it to renounce its Christian cultural heritage. Similarly, the modern state under the rule of law is not completely neutral in religious matters or able to act completely independently of all religious influence; indeed, such abstinence would be counterproductive.[6] For instance, if the state refused to coordinate (multi-confessional) facilities for pastoral care in prisons, it would effectively compel inmates to lead a largely atheist life while they served their sentence.[7] In so doing, the state would itself become a proponent of atheism. Hence, it is reasonable that the requirement for states to consistently maintain religious neutrality should be subject to certain limits.

1.2. No legal entitlement to ordination

To explore the significance of the law for gender equality in religious communities and Churches, in the following we shall present further connections and correlations between religion and law.

First, a clarification is necessary. The declaration *Inter Insigniores* of the Sacred Congregation for the Doctrine of the Faith states: "Moreover, and above all, to consider the ministerial priesthood as a human right would be to misjudge its nature completely: baptism does not confer any personal title to public ministry within the Church."[8]

---

4 See *Huber*, p. 254 f.; regarding the gap between Church and modernity see also *Nagl-Docekal*, pp. 92 ff.

5 *Hafner*, Religionsfreiheit, p. 125.

6 *Sahlfeld*, pp. 79 ff.

7 *Hafner*, Trennung, p. 241; for further examples see *Campenhausen / de Wall*, p. 349 (at the bottom).

8 Sacred Congregation for the Doctrine of the Faith, *Inter Insigniores*, 15 October 1976, published by *Gross*, Frauenordination, pp. 11 ff., 23.

The Roman Catholic Church does not recognise an individual right to ordination. However, one may not conclude from this that because men, too, do not have an individual right to ordination the non-admission of women to the ministerial priesthood is not discrimination against women.[9] The fact that men do not have an individual right either, neither redresses nor mitigates the exclusion of women from the ministerial priesthood.[10]

The inequality is a consequence not of the act of ordination, but of the determination of the prerequisites that have to be fulfilled for ordination. Even if it is *not* a consequence of *can. 1024 CIC – "Only a baptised male validly receives sacred ordination"* – that every Roman Catholic man (who so desires) is eligible for sacred ordination,[11] the provision nonetheless specifies that an ordained person must be a man; therefore, women are excluded from ordination without exception and a priori.

Because existing canon law holds that women "on account of their gender alone cannot be ordained",[12] non-admission to the priesthood and the prerequisites that expressly exclude one gender from ordination constitute discrimination.

By posing the question: "Do women have a *right* to the priesthood?"[13] there is an assumption in theological ethics of a "structural right to women's priesthood in the Church",[14] which, however, is "not the same as a personal, individual right".[15] The crucial argument rests "on the theory of justice, [according to which] offices and positions [must] be open to all on the basis of equal opportunity".[16] This also holds for the Roman Catholic Church, insofar as it seeks to act in accordance with what is "morally correct"[17]. As "an institution created by God with our involvement, the structures [of the Church can] not lag behind the inescapable conditions of institutional justice"[18].

Accordingly, the issue of equality arises not from the existence of an individual right or lack thereof, but from the negative formulation of exclusion.

States that guarantee religious freedom have a substantial body of jurisprudence covering a wide range of cases concerning religion[19] – unlike states with an

---

9 See *Hallensleben*, pp. 288 ff.

10 Also *Hafner*, Religionsfreiheit, pp. 152 f.

11 For this concept in Catholic teaching see *Brosi*, pp. 148 ff.

12 *Hafner*, Religionsfreiheit, p. 153.

13 *Mieth*, pp. 97 ff.

14 *Mieth*, p. 99.

15 *Mieth*, loc. cit.

16 *Mieth*, loc. cit.

17 *Mieth*, loc. cit.

18 *Mieth*, loc. cit.

19 Selection of court rulings pertaining to religious issues:
– On 22. December 1921 the Swiss Federal Supreme Court ruled against an amendment to the Constitution of the Swiss Protestant Church, which would have allowed women to be elected

established or state religion or without religious freedom and that deny individuals the right not to observe the state religion.[20]

The decisions of the European Court of Human Rights illustrate the spectrum of case law on the freedom of religion, as guaranteed by Art. 9 of the European Convention on Human Rights (ECHR).[21]

The Court has ruled on religion-related aspects of lifestyle (head covering, nutrition), on issues of religion related to public schools and prisons and on the position of religious minorities.[22] These cases deal for the most part with questions of the religious freedom of individuals, in other words, the individual's manifest-

---

as pastors (FSC 47 I 484; http://www.servat.unibe.ch/dfr/pdf/c1047484.pdf, accessed 4 October 2016).

– Decision of the German Federal Constitutional Court of 4 June 1985 concerning church criteria for evaluating a contractual duty of loyalty (http://www.servat.unibe.ch/dfr/bv070138.html, accessed 4 October 2016).

– Decision of the European Court of Human Rights of 23 September 2010 in Obst vs. Germany (adultery as an extraordinary ground for dismissal according to the self-understanding of the church; http://hudoc.echr.coe.int/sites/fra/pages/search.aspx?i=001-100463, accessed 4 October 2016).

– Decision of the Swiss Federal Supreme Court of 18 December 2002 concerning leaving the church I, FSC 129 I 68 (www.bger.ch, accessed 4 October 2016).

– Decision of the Swiss Federal Supreme Court of 16 November 2007 concerning leaving the church II, FSC 134 I 75 (www.bger.ch, accessed 4 October 2016)

– Decision of the Swiss Federal Supreme Court of 9 July 2012 concerning leaving the church III, 2C_406/2011 (http://www.bger.ch/index/juridiction/jurisdiction-inherit-template/jurisdiction-recht/jurisdiction-recht-urteile2000.htm, accessed 9 July 2013).

– Decision of the Cantonal Court of the Canton of Basel-Landschaft of 5 September 2007 concerning the Roman Catholic community of Röschenz (http://www.baselland.ch/006-htm.275370.0.html, accessed 4 October 2016).

– Decision of the Cologne Regional Court of 7 May 2012 concerning the circumcision of a four-year-old boy (http://www.justiz.nrw.de/nrwe/lgs/koeln/lg_koeln/j2012/151_Ns_169_11_Urteil_20120507.html, accessed 4 October 2016). See also the case overview in *Sahlfeld*, pp. 84 ff.; an overview of decisions of the Swiss Federal Supreme Court and individual cantons concerning religious issues is published by the Institute of Law and Religion of the University of Fribourg: www.unifr.ch/religionsrecht (accessed 4 October 2016).

20 A contradiction arises if such states are member states of the United States (UN); Art. 18 of the Universal Declaration of Human Rights guarantees the right to freedom of religion.

21 Art. 9 ECHR: Freedom of thought, conscience and religion.
1) Everyone has the right to freedom of thought, conscience and religion; this right includes freedom to change his religion or belief and freedom, either alone or in community with others and in public or private, to manifest his religion or belief, in worship, teaching, practice and observance.
2) Freedom to manifest one's religion or beliefs shall be subject only to such limitations as are prescribed by law and are necessary in a democratic society in the interests of public safety, for the protection of public order health or morals, or for the protection of the rights and freedoms of others.

22 See *Kraus*, Religionsfreiheit, pp. 190 ff.

ation of religion either alone or in community with others.[23] The primary duty of the Court is to determine the scope that the state (or the individual member states of the ECHR) must grant individuals to exercise their religious freedom.

Less common are decisions in which the plaintiff is a religious community. In one such case the Court expressly recognised that the organisation came within the protection afforded by freedom of religion.[24] In a decision of 26 October 2000 (*Hasan and Chaush vs. Bulgaria*) the Court ruled in a case involving the claim of two parallel Muslim communities to religious supremacy in which the then Bulgarian government officially recognised the traditionalists. The state ignored the other religious community. The registration by the state of only one of the two religious communities would have meant the end of the term of office of the chief mufti of the non-registered faith group and the loss of the religious leadership of the Muslim religious community, which they had exercised up to that point. The Court interpreted this as an arbitrary *violation* of the *right to religious freedom* as the registration of only one of two religious groups lacked an adequate basis in statutory law and the opposing party had been denied a hearing.[25]

At this point we need to briefly examine the *terminology* used below as, owing to the on-going academic debate, the terms are not always used uniformly in legal doctrine and jurisprudence. At issue are the different aspects of religious freedom, i.e., *individual, collective and corporative religious freedom*, religious communities' *right to self-determination*, and the differences between religious communities *organised under private law* and those *recognised under public law*.

The reference point for individual and collective religious freedom is whether the fundamental right is invoked by an individual or by the religious community. The latter is the case, for instance, when the religious community draws up regulations that apply to the whole group that can in a conflict be legally enforced.[26] In this respect, one could present the issue of the non-admission of women's ordination in the Roman Catholic Church as a conflict over fundamental rights between individual and collective religious freedom, provided that a single woman theologian is willing to stand up as an advocate for women's ordination against her religious community, which supports the opposite view. In the following analysis, though, the issue is treated as a conflict over fundamental rights between gender

---

[23] Here one may also speak of collective religious freedom. Collective religious freedom is the joint exercise of individual rights. In addition, if it is possible in a state based on the rule of law for a religious community to claim corporative rights, one speaks of corporative religious freedom (see *Kraus*, Staatskirchenrecht, pp. 95 ff; *Loretan*, vol. 1, p. 114).

[24] *Kraus*, Religionsfreiheit, pp. 190 ff.

[25] ECHR 2000-XI 117 ff. = ILM 40 (2001), 12 ff.; the decision is in the electronic collection of the Court reports (HUDOC, Human Rights DOCumentation, http://hudoc.echr.coe.int/, search words: "Hasan and Chaush"; accessed 4 October 2016).

[26] See *Hafner*, Religionsfreiheit, p. 143.

equality and religious freedom, as the intention is to present the topic not as the issue in an individual case, but as a structural issue of fundamental rights (equality vs. religious freedom).

Corporative religious freedom means the right of the religious community to perceive itself as a holder of fundamental rights. Associated with this is the question of religious self-determination. Whereas in Switzerland the existence of a right to self-determination has not been fully clarified, it is assumed that in general German law grants religious communities, independent of their status under public or private law, far-reaching corporative rights and a right to self-determination, especially as Art. 140/137 III of the Basic Law of the Federal Republic of Germany[27] lays down that: "Each religious body regulates and administers its affairs independently within the limits of general laws."[28]

Finally, there is the difference between the religious communities organised under private law and those recognised under public law. The public recognition of religious communities assumes a certain obligation to respect fundamental rights, which at the same time correspondingly restricts the communities' right to self-determination or their corporative rights.[29] In contrast, the right of religious communities organised under private law to appeal to religious freedom is practically unrestricted. That said, they have to be prepared for the eventuality that their fundamental rights can conflict with the fundamental rights of others.

Despite this complex state of affairs, a case of conflict between fundamental rights will be resolved by weighing up the competing interests between the principles of gender equality and religion freedom. As this question of priority is the focus of this paper, in each case we shall proceed with the variant that is most favourable to the religious communities (appeal to religious freedom by the religious community as an expression of the right to self-determination).

1.3. Law and religion

Another point of contact between law and religion in the evolution of the law (in the west) is the gradual emergence of constitutional guarantees of fundamental rights. The basic concern of modern concepts of human rights is not the efficient and smoothly functioning technical procedure for drawing up and applying legal regulations that facilitate coexistence in complex societies with as little conflict as possible. Rather, the concept of human rights developed out of the intellectual history of a view of man in which individual persons were finally recognised as rational beings with enforceable rights which enabled them to act on the basis of

27 Art. 137 III is a provision adopted from the (Weimar) Constitution of 1919.

28 *Hafner*, Religionsfreiheit, p. 146; *Campenhausen / de Wall*, pp. 99 ff.

29 *Hafner*, Religionsfreiheit, pp. 145, 148 ff.

reason. The numerous sources of inspiration for this intellectual history include, in addition to the philosophical concepts of antiquity, the Judeo-Christian tradition, which itself had adopted many elements of those philosophical schools.[30] Thus, ideas of the Stoic School such as respect for others or the view of the dignity of each and every individual were a significant source for modern thinking about human rights. Other important impulses include Judeo-Christian teachings on charity and the assumption that man is made in God's own likeness.[31] Despite many failures in practical implementation and the catastrophic transgressions in human history committed in the name of religion, the idea of human rights is "in many respects rooted in western Christian church traditions"[32] and the fundamental Jewish and Christian values can be regarded as "important prerequisites for human rights"[33].

Thus, the approaches of law and religion in respect of fundamental rights are rooted in a shared history of ideas. If primacy is accorded to state law, this initially means only that the state decides whether it may consider circumstances that lead to a conflict as a case for the law, before subsequently proceeding to resolve it in a formal process. This does not mean that religious communities simply lose out. Rather, religious freedom must be such that religious communities in a secular polity can as far as possible act effectively without (state) restrictions.

1.4. Constellations of conflict in the field of religion

Three case studies will serve to illustrate the need to find solutions within the religious sphere to legal questions with a theological dimension. If the parties involved have different interests, such conflict constellations may give rise to contradictions and dilemmas. If these situations arise in areas that are regulated or affected by state law, the state will have to address the relationship between religion and state norms. Finally, the state will have to make a binding decision to resolve an existing conflict.

The chosen case studies, all of which are fictitious and without precedent, involve the Roman Catholic Church because this religious community has an explicit canonical rule that excludes women from the spiritual office of priesthood. The legal considerations can also be correspondingly applied to other religious communities that exclude one gender from access to spiritual offices.

In *case study 1* a prospective female theology student applies for admission to a seminary with a view to combining her theological studies with specialised

---

30 On the history of human rights see *Spenlé/Mugier*, pp. 43 ff.; *Wolgast*, pp. 11 ff.

31 See *Huber*, p. 234, *Kirchschläger*, p. 344.

32 *Hafner*, Kirchen, p. 219.

33 *Spenlé/Mugier*, p. 50.

training for the priesthood. The seminary authorities refuse her admission on the grounds that the requirement under canon law that candidates for the priesthood have to be male makes it impossible for her to be a candidate for the priesthood. Therefore, it is clear from the outset that her studies would be pointless and, hence, her application is rejected.

In her submission to the court the applicant states that she is aware that she does not satisfy the gender prerequisite for the priesthood under the existing law. However, in view of the rapid decline in the number of male candidates for the priesthood, it could be expected that the gender requirement for the appointment of priests would be qualified in the future, either by opening up the diaconate to women or through some other solution sanctioned by the Catholic hierarchy for regulating admission to the priesthood. The applicant also produces spiritual and scientific arguments for her desire to combine her theological studies with seminary training. She says she is convinced that the study of theology demands an exceptional degree of "education and training, human maturity and spiritual depth".[34] The only feasible way to achieve this is by combining her studies with the communal experience of seminary life. Accordingly, seriously motivated female theology students should be allowed to apply for admission to the seminary. She explains: "Here they live as a community. Living together with like-minded people should help"[35] one to establish a meaningful balance between studies, research and prayer "to prepare oneself for the church in all its diversity",[36] to familiarise oneself with the structures of the official Church and, last but not least, to intensify one's joy in theology in a community of kindred spirits.

The seminary director requests an opinion from the theological faculty with which the seminary cooperates on whether there are theological grounds *for* admitting the student. The theology professor commissioned to provide an expert opinion concludes that male theology students do not have a right to admission to the seminary either. On the contrary, prior to admission (male) applicants are examined to verify that they had the aptitude necessary for future candidates for the priesthood. However, because the applicant is female, she cannot be admitted to the priesthood; hence, there is no question of her taking such a psychological aptitude test. Accordingly, there are no grounds for further evaluation of her reasons for admission to the seminary. In a phone call from the secretariat of the seminary the applicant is informed that she will receive an official letter of rejection from the faculty of theology. The communication from the dean of the faculty of theology informs her that her application has been rejected "for theological reasons".

34 Quoted from the home page of the seminary in Chur (http://www.priesterseminar-chur.ch, status as of March 2013).

35 Loc. cit.

36 Loc. cit.

The letter cites the opinion of the theology professor, which does not even fill an A4 page. The applicant intends to contest the letter of rejection from the faculty of theology in court.

In *case study 2* a female parish administrator is in charge of a number of parishes as part of a team with a parish priest. Once a month the parish priest, assisted by his female colleague, celebrates a Eucharistic liturgy in the largest – a centrally located – church. Apart from this, their full-time jobs are practically identical. Duties that can be carried out only by a priest are attended to by the parish priest: Anointing of the Sick and hearing (the rare) individual confessions.[37] The female parish administrator is also responsible for representing the parish in matters beyond pastoral care and attends meetings of the bodies that deal with relations between church and state.

The incumbents are of the same age and studied at the same university. The parish priest completed an additional year of studies at the papal Gregoriana University, but left before acquiring a diploma. The female parish administrator did a theological internship in a Brazilian favela and during her theology degree completed a competence course in ecumenical and interreligious dialogue. Because he is ordained, the parish priest's salary is 15 percent higher than that of the female parish administrator. She intends to bring an action for equal pay in court.

In *case study 3* the protagonist is a female parish administrator in a permanent position. She was initially elected, and subsequently thrice re-elected, by the parish in fair and proper elections, with prior approval of the Church hierarchy. Before her fourth re-election (after 15 years in office) she was ordained as a priest "*contra legem*".[38] The members of her parish are informed of this and continue to attend her church services. Since her ordination she has continued to work as female parish administrator and once a month presides at a service that includes Eucharistic liturgy.

---

[37] On the ecclesiastical authorisation of clerics and lay persons see *Brosi*, pp. 159 ff.

[38] The concept was introduced to describe the ordination of seven Catholic women as priests on a ship in the Danube on 29 June 2002. Under the title of *Ordination "contra legem" als möglicher Ausweg und Impuls für Reform (Ordination* contra legem *as a possible solution and stimulus for reform)* Ida Raming writes: "After 40 years of arguing orally and in writing for admission to the diaconate and presbyterate – ever since the Second Vatican Council (1962–1965) – to which the church leadership in the Vatican reacted with an increasingly implacable no, these women recognised that it is, unfortunately, impossible to find a solution to the issue of female ordination that is consistent with the ecclesiastical system, e.g. in 'dialogue' with the Church hierarchy. (…) Accordingly, in 2002 seven women from Austria and Germany decided to act in breach of Church law (can. 1024) and the underlying doctrine, i.e., for ordination *contra legem*." *Hainz McGrath/Meehan/Raming,* pp. 10 f.; *Raming/Müller,* pp. 68 f.; *Müller/Raming,* pp. 73 ff. The lawyer Gertrud Heinzelmann was also of the view that a courageous bishop should start to ordain women so as to establish a succession. See *Judith Stofer*, Interview mit Gertrud Heinzelmann: Wer weiht die erste Frau? DAZ, 16 August 1995.

In a series of discussions with the female parish administrator the Church authorities demand that she re-establish her previous lawful understanding of ministry and abstain from actions that require legitimate ordination. She has not been excommunicated because the Church authorities hope they can reach an amicable solution.

The parish holds the election on the appointed date. At the parish meeting the (only) candidate, the parish administrator, is re-elected unanimously without abstentions. The announcement of the election result in the parish's official publication referred to the elected person as "[female] priest".

Thereupon the elected cantonal church council declares the election invalid because it contravenes canon law. Both the parish council and the successful candidate intend to contest the order in court.

Despite the different circumstances, these three case studies have several points in common:

- Common to all three cases is the treatment that a woman must expect solely because she is a woman. Because women cannot become priests, a female student of Catholic theology is refused admission to a seminary. In the second case study a woman is not employed at the same salary level as her team colleague because she cannot show she is ordained, a status reserved to men alone. In the third case study the election of a woman is declared invalid because she ignored the provision of canon law that women may not be admitted to ordination.
- The parties in each of the three case studies claim mutually exclusive fundamental freedoms. In their favour, the women affected have the ban on gender discrimination or the right to gender equality (cases 1, 2 and 3) and the right to equal pay (case 2). The Church for its part can cite freedom of religion or religious communities' right to self-determination (cases 1, 2 and 3). Case 2 is peculiar in that the issue of equal pay involved here is the only case that involves a fundamental right with direct third-party effect (also available against communities *organised under private law*). In the case of equal pay the legislator has settled the conflict over the fundamental rights between equality on the one hand and private autonomy and economic freedom on the other at the constitutional level in favour of equal pay. In the specific individual case the issue to be decided is whether the work in question is "equal" or "of equal value", in other words whether the legal prerequisite for equal pay is fulfilled.
- In the context of the specific case analysis[39] it has to be determined whether and to what extent the case can be tried in a public court.[40] Further, it has to be determined whether these legal cases involve a so-called *conflict of fundamental*

[39] See chap. 4.

[40] This is tied up with the question of whether the three model cases are justiciable, i.e. whether they are capable of being determined by a state court.

rights. In classic constitutional cases one or more private individuals confront the state. The function of fundamental rights is primarily defensive with the intention of protecting private individuals (individuals or groups) against government intervention. Hence, the state is in the position of the interfering party with respect to a private individual. In a *conflict* of fundamental rights, on the other hand, the question is whether a private individual or a private institution "in the exercise of their fundamental freedom affects the fundamental rights of another private individual. In contrast to cases in which fundamental rights constitute a legal defence, the violator of fundamental rights is not the state, but another private individual (...)."[41] The affected party's defence does not, however, directly affect the private interfering party, but is mediated through the state. Therefore, a conflict of fundamental rights must, on principle, be dealt with in a court of law.[42]

41 *Martin*, p. 30; *Spielmann*, pp. 24 f. There is a distinction between competition between fundamental rights and a conflict of fundamental rights: whereas the former exists when the circumstances of a case may be subsumed under several fundamental rights, a conflict of fundamental rights exists if the spheres protected by different fundamental rights clash or collide (see *Häfelin/Haller/Keller/Thurnherr*, note 318).

42 *Martin*, p. 30; *Isensee*, notes 4 ff.; *Unruh*, pp. 21 f.

Facts	In *case study 1* a theology student wants to be admitted to special training for priests to complete her studies; her application for admission is rejected on the grounds that she can never exercise the priestly office because of her gender; the training is therefore pointless.	In *case study 2* a female parish administrator and priest are in charge of several parishes as a team. Duties reserved to a priest are tended to by the priest: Eucharistic liturgy, anointing of the sick, and hearing confessions of individuals. The female parish administrator is responsible for representing the parish in external matters (including membership of committees). For the rest their duties are largely identical. The priest's salary is 15 percent higher than that of the female parish administrator.	In *case study 3* the protagonist is a female parish administrator. Her initial election and three subsequent re-elections were conducted fairly and properly by the parish with the prior approval of the Church hierarchy. Before her fourth re-election (after 15 years in office) she was ordained as a priest *contra legem* and once a month celebrates a church service with Eucharistic liturgy. Despite several warnings, she has not been excommunicated by the official Church. She is re-elected unanimously by the parish. In the parish's official publication she is referred to as "[female] priest". The elected cantonal church council then declared the election invalid because it contravened canon law.

Conflicting fundamental rights	Claim to equality of the (prospective) female theology student vs. freedom of religion, self-determination of the Church / religious community	In the case of equal pay the legislator has already settled the conflict over the fundamental rights between equality on the one hand and private autonomy and economic freedom on the other at the constitutional level in favour of equal pay. In the specific individual case the issue to be decided is whether the work in question is "equal" or "of equal value".	Right to equality of the female priest *contra legem* vs. freedom of religion, self-determination of the Church / religious community
Parties	(Prospective) female theology student vs. seminary authorities in conjunction with the theological faculty	Female parish administrator vs. employer, i.e., the Church or the elected cantonal church council[43]	Female priest *contra legem* vs. elected cantonal church council and the official Church

The question of whether a state court of law would accept these cases if presented with the facts cannot be answered with absolute certainty. Given the aforementioned substantial body of jurisprudence on religious freedom at both the national and international levels (e.g. European Court of Human Rights) the probability is high.

1.5. Precedent: court of law corrects bishop

One particular decision deserves special mention in view of its potential as a precedent, namely that of the cantonal court of Canton Basel-Landschaft of 5 September 2007 in the case of the Roman Catholic community of Röschenz.

[43] Switzerland does not have a uniform statutory system governing church-state relations; instead there are 26 in part very different cantonal systems (for an overview see Brosi, pp. 252 ff.). In Canton Neuchâtel churches and religious communities are organised under private law; the Fédération catholique romaine neuchâteloise, which is incorporated as an association, is responsible for the payment of salaries (see also Kraus, Staatskirchenrecht, pp. 298, 300).

The facts of the case are as follows: on 1 January 1999 F.S. assumed the function of parish administrator in the Catholic community of Röschenz. In 2003 and 2004 F.S. criticised the local leadership of the Catholic Church in a newspaper interview and in a reader's letter. After a number of meetings failed to produce agreement, the bishop revoked the priest's canonical mission. Thereupon, on 6 June 2006 the executive body of the Roman Catholic Regional Church in Canton Basel-Landschaft (hereinafter "elected cantonal church council") sent a directive, referred to as an order, to the community of Röschenz, directing it to "terminate the employment contract with Mr F.S. when this order becomes final, subject to the usual period of notice". On 14 June 2006 the community lodged an appeal against this directive with the Basel-Landschaft cantonal court.

The court upheld the community's appeal and set aside the directive of elected cantonal church council. As a corporation under public law the elected cantonal church council is not bound to blindly enforce the bishop's preliminary decision if this was reached through a procedure that violated the priest's fundamental rights. The latter had not received a fair hearing, nor were the grounds for the revocation of his licence substantiated.[44] In the (internal Church) procedure of revoking the canonical mission the bishop has a duty to observe the right to a fair hearing in court because the bishop's decision directly affects regulations under public law (including implementation by the elected cantonal church council). Thus, the bishop's decision to revoke the licence is part of the ruling of the cantonal church. Therefore, if the bishop's decision concerns an employment contract, as in the case of F.S., i.e., "is intended to have direct and immediate effects in matters subject to public law"[45], at the time he made his decision the bishop was already bound by the general principles of procedure.

The decision of the cantonal court addresses the relationship between corporative freedom of religion or the Church's right to self-determination and the fundamental rights of the individual in question. It reads:[46]

With regard to the issue of an order to terminate an employment contract with a parish administrator a preliminary examination of the decision to revoke the canonical mission

44 Under canon law the Church should have followed similar procedural rules (see cann. 1742 and 1745 CIC, which govern a parish priest's rights to a fair hearing and of access to documents in proceedings to remove him from office).

45 Decision of the cantonal court of the Canton of Basel-Landschaft in the case of the Roman Catholic parish of Röschenz, 5 September 2007, consideration 13 (http://www.baselland.ch/006-htm.275370.0.html, accessed 4 October 2016).

46 In the following quote references to further reading and other references are omitted for reasons of readability [indicated by (...)]. Art. 35 para. 2 SFC reads: "Any person who performs public duties is bound by the fundamental rights and has a duty to contribute to their realisation." On the terms corporative religious freedom and right to self-determination see *Kraus,* Staatskirchenrecht, pp. 95 ff.

must – as the lower instance initially correctly determined – examine whether the order, if it is invoked as the sole ground for dismissal, violates fundamental rights in substance. That said, in each individual case this examination must weigh up the balance between the corporative religious freedom and the fundamental rights of the party concerned (...). Insofar as the cantonal church as a statutory corporation of public law exercises derived jurisdiction, it is, in accordance with Art. 35 para. 2 SFC, bound by the fundamental rights and has a duty to contribute to their realisation. That said, whereas in the case of the termination of an employment contract the constitution requires the cantonal church to observe the fundamental rights of others, it also at the same time recognises the Church's, parish's and cantonal Church's fundamental right to freedom of religion, which they can invoke in accordance with teaching and practice (...). This raises the possibility of a conflict between the corporative dimension of religious freedom derived from the right to self-determination of the religious communities and the fundamental rights to which pastoral carers are entitled, for instance their freedom of belief and conscience, freedom of expression and personal liberty (...). The conflict of rights must be resolved by weighing up interests through the application of the principle of proportionality in accordance with the facts of each individual case and the conflicting fundamental rights. This means that in all situations of conflict between the right to self-determination of the religious communities and the constitutionally guaranteed rights of third parties a proportionate allocation of the legally protected interests in question must be achieved through practical concordance, ensuring in the process as optimal an expression as possible of all of the involved interests and rights. The complete negation of the one or other constitutional guarantee is to be avoided as far as possible.

The structure of the cantonal court's argumentation in its decision on the Catholic community of Röschenz should not be underestimated. Although no official church representative – neither the bishop nor the disciplined parish administrator in person as plaintiff – appeared in court, i.e., the opposing parties at the proceedings in the cantonal court were statutory church-state institutions (elected cantonal church council and the community), the decision had a considerable impact on an autonomous act of the Church: the bishop's revocation of the canonical mission was effectively suspended.[47] At the same time, the court's decision clearly demonstrates that in a conflict of fundamental rights the nature of the balance of interests lies in defining a just balance, thereby avoiding arbitrarily or one-sidedly giving one fundamental right priority over another.[48]

A conflict of fundamental rights exists when the fundamental freedoms of two (non-state) parties to a conflict are in a relationship of mutual tension. The

47 Consideration 11 of the decision states: "Therefore the revocation of the canonical mission, valid and legal at most under canon law, qualifies as insignificant for the organs of the Cantonal Church that are bound by fundamental rights. Owing to the insignificance of the revocation of the canonical mission, which has relevance only within the Church, there is no obligation to terminate the employment contract between the parish and its parish administrator."

48 Consideration 13 of the cantonal court deals with consideration of the diverging interests.

protection of the one position means that the ability of the other party to exercise its fundamental freedom is restricted or denied.[49] To find a just balance in an individual case a procedure based on the principle of practical concordance is applied.[50] The goal of this optimisation process is "a fair balance between all constitutionally protected interests involved"[51], whereby the contradictory interests must be weighed up in a way that shows the greatest possible consideration of both sides' interests to ensure that both positions suffer as little impairment as possible.[52] Therefore, the concern or the interest of one party should not be rashly exaggerated at the expense of the other. Rather, it is a question of taking into account all existing interests and circumstances in a case and finding a proportionate balance between the opposing positions. The principle of practical concordance does not state what the proportionate solution is.[53] The conflict of fundamental rights must be resolved by finding a compromise. The opposing interests of both parties must be carefully weighed up so as to ultimately establish a balance between the one and the other (impaired) fundamental right. This balance must be as considerate as possible of the interests of both sides.[54]

Insofar as religious laws include references to gender differences, the differences should be examined to determine whether they are rooted in gender roles that originated in or were perpetuated by religious traditions. If so, such gender roles may not serve as objective and justifiable reasons for normative distinctions in religious laws.[55]

1.6. Individual and corporative religious freedom

Despite the aforementioned points of contact and interfaces between law and religion, the question of what the law has to do with religion has still not been answered in full. One valid standpoint is that law and religion are two different spheres without points of contact and not comparable.[56] However, if individual cases involve fields of conflict with religious references, because of its monopoly

49 *Biaggini/Gächter/Kiener,* § 30 n. 86.

50 See *Martin*, pp. 224 ff. The concept of practical concordance was introduced by *Richard Bäumlin*, see *Kley*, p. 214; on the application of practical concordance see also *Hesse*, n. 317 f.

51 *Martin,* p. 224.

52 *Martin*, including further bibliographical references, p. 225.

53 *Martin*, p. 226.

54 *Martin*, p. 226.

55 *Sullivan*, p. 855

56 *Campenhausen / de Wall* simply state that "equality before the law within the religious communities cannot be based on the argument that Art. 3 of the Basic Law of the Federal Republic of Germany gives women a right to equality in spiritual offices". This statement is unsubstantiated. Therefore, it is unclear whether the right does not exist because the legal prerequisites do not exist or because the religion can claim a legal vacuum (*Campenhausen / de Wall*, p. 115).

of the law the state under the rule of law is not only called upon, but also has a duty, to set binding standards to resolve the conflict. The means of conflict solution is the legal procedure that concludes with a legally binding act – a court decision if the parties to a conflict go to court. In other words, the law comes into play only if the religiously referenced conflict cannot be solved otherwise.

An alternative method of dealing with a dispute is for the involved parties to reach a solution on their own, whereby the problem solving can be structured in such a way that not only the specific individual case is settled, but other similar cases (or disputes) can be avoided from the start. As this, however, presumes that the parties involved are capable of qualifying their own standpoints, autonomous conflict management of this nature is not always feasible for the parties involved.

In many cases the parties involved are not equally powerful, with the result that the playing field is not level. If one of the parties is a "power centre" – an economically potent institution or a socially influential institution with a corresponding infrastructure – the opposing individual will have difficulty prevailing, no matter how strong his arguments are. The constellation resembles the situation in which the individual citizen is restricted in the exercise of his constitutionally guaranteed freedoms by an (overbearing) state. In contrast to the state, however, the private power centre does not have to assume a position of neutrality: it can exploit its position of power without restriction. This in turn makes it difficult for the opposing side – the individual – to voluntarily enter into a conflict procedure that, on account of the parties' relative strengths, is unlikely to be decided in his favour.

In addition, a procedure to balance opposing interests requires an objective weighting of the arguments presented by both sides. For example, in the procedure of practical concordance the fundamental rights of the victim are accorded greater weight if the interfering party not only impairs the victim's ability to exercise his fundamental rights, but renders it completely impossible.[57] This constellation exists when specific persons are denied admission to a religious office solely on the grounds of gender,[58] as in the case of the Roman Catholic priesthood. Given this state of affairs, any attempt to find a balance of interests must take into account the fact that all female theologians in this denomination are deprived of their fundamental right not be discriminated against on account of their gender.

---

57 *Martin*, p. 251.

58 The rule that certain religious ministries (dispensing the sacraments, celebrating the Eucharistic liturgy, etc.) can only be performed by a priest also excludes lay theologians, in other words, men who do not want to live in celibacy and are not ordained. Women, however, are affected particularly severely, as they do not have a choice solely on the grounds of gender – even if they are living celibate lives as nuns. See *Strahm/Rudolf*, pp. 38 f.

This fundamental right cannot be qualified because of its constitutional strength,[59] which renders the balance of interests even more complicated.

The issue of denying or de facto severely restricting the access of women to important religious ministries – whether the rabbinate in Judaism, leading religious positions in Islam or ordination in Roman Catholic Christianity – is often presented as a conflict between individual and corporative freedom of religion. Characteristic of corporative religious freedom is the right of leaders of a religious community in a secular state under the rule of law to assert their constitutional right to religious freedom, both against the threat of interference by the state as well as in cases of conflict between private individuals in which the state has to mediate. If a woman who is a victim of a discriminatory religious practice claims her rights under gender equality, this is an expression on the one hand of her individual right to equality and to religious freedom. In the wider sense, though, hers is also a claim at the structural level inasmuch as the denial of equality (and religious freedom) affects the entire collective, in other words all female members of the religious community that are theoretically or de facto affected by the same discrimination.[60] The group of female members within the religious community can also be viewed as the object of corporative religious freedom. This freedom is infringed at least indirectly if the state fails to fulfil its duty of protection and ensure that the principle of equality is enforced in the religious sphere.[61]

1.7. Changes in the role of women in the religious sphere

Developments in international feminism since the 1960s[62] have affected all areas of life, including religion,[63] – whereby theological scholarship has long grappled with Church teaching on the non-admission of women to the ministerial priesthood.[64] Practically every country has signed and ratified the UN Convention on the

59 *Hafner*, Religionsfreiheit, p. 152.

60 See *Sullivan*, p. 856.

61 The Convention on the Elimination of All Forms of Discrimination against Women (CEDAW) does not expressly mention the religious sphere. The work of the CEDAW, however, is in principle not restricted to dealing only with state-inspired discrimination against women (see *Freeman* et al., pp. 87 ff.).

62 The modern women's movement started in the years leading up to the First World War.

63 However, we should not forget the significant role played by individuals. The Swiss lawyer Gertrud Heinzelmann (1914–1999) acquired a reputation early on as a church critic. In a petition submitted to the Second Vatican Council in 1962 she called on the Pope to allow the ordination of women, see *Heinzelmann*, pp. 90 ff.; *Kopp*, pp. 144 ff.; *Brodbeck*, pp. 222 ff.; *Brodbeck/Domhardt/Stofer*, pp. 103 ff.; *Gössmann* et al., p. 457; *Stofer*, pp. 172 ff. The original text of the petition is available at http://www.womenpriests.org/de/deutsch/heinzel2.asp, accessed 4 October 2016.

64 *Demel*, p. 86.

Elimination of All Forms of Discrimination against Women (CEDAW).[65] The prohibition on debate about the priestly ordination of women contained in the apostolic letter of 1994 has remained largely ineffective. Rather, the issue of women's ordination is a regular subject of discussion in academic and socio-political circles.[66] The former general social consensus on the historical, patriarchal definition

65 However, numerous individual signatories have issued declarations and reservations; see http://treaties.un.org; heading: Overview/Status of Multilateral Treaties deposited with the Secretary-General/Chapter IV: Human Rights/8.; accessed 6 April 2013. The USA signed the Convention on 17 July 1980, but has not yet ratified it.

66 On 28 September 2014 members of the regional Roman Catholic churches of the Swiss cantons of Basel-Stadt and Basel-Landschaft voted to amend their respective ecclesiastical constitutions under public law to include the following stipulation: the two cantonal churches must propose to the church authorities that access to priesthood should be possible irrespective of gender and marital status. In most Swiss cantons members of the Roman Catholic Church are subject to two legal systems: global canon law as stipulated in the Codex Iuris Canonici, and the local, democratic ecclesiastical law, based on an ecclesiastical constitution, modelled after the cantonal public law system.

A selection of literature on women's ordination (in the Roman Catholic Church) since the Pope's definitive decision of 1994: *Hanna-Renate Laurien*, Abgeschrieben? Plädoyer für eine faire Diskussion über das Priestertum der Frau, Basel 1995; *Manfred Hauke*, Die Problematik um das Frauenpriestertum vor dem Hintergrund der Schöpfungs- und Erlösungsordnung, Paderborn 1995; *Walter Gross* (ed.), Frauenordination, Stand der Diskussion in der Katholischen Kirche, Munich 1996; *Felix Hafner/Denise Buser*, Frauenordination via Gleichstellungsgesetz? Die Anwendbarkeit des Gleichstellungsgesetzes auf die Dienstverhältnisse in der römisch-katholischen Kirche, in: Aktuelle Juristische Praxis, vol. 5 (1996), pp. 1207 ff.; *Ida Raming* et al. (eds), Zur Priesterin berufen: Gott sieht nicht auf das Geschlecht, Zeugnisse römisch-katholischer Frauen, Thaur/Vienna/Munich 1998; *Dorothea Reininger*, Diakonat der Frau in der Einen Kirche, Diskussionen, Entscheidungen und pastoral-praktische Erfahrungen in der christlichen Ökumene und ihr Beitrag zur römisch-katholischen Diskussion, Ostfildern 1999; *Gerhard Ludwig Müller* (ed.), Frauen in der Kirche, Eigensein und Mitverantwortung, Würzburg 1999; *Denise Buser/Adrian Loretan* (eds), Gleichstellung der Geschlechter und die Kirchen, Ein Beitrag zur menschenrechtlichen und ökumenischen Diskussion, Fribourg 1999; *Jane H.Bayes/Nayereh Tohidi* (eds), Globalization, Gender and Religion, The Politics of Women's Rights in Catholic and Muslim Contexts, Basingstoke 2001; *John Wijngaards*, The Ordination of Women in the Catholic Church, Unmasking a Cuckoo's Egg Tradition, Delhi 2002; *Ida Raming*, Priesteramt der Frau – Geschenk Gottes für eine erneuerte Kirche, Münster 2002; *Helen Schüngel-Straumann*, Anfänge feministischer Exegese, Münster 2002, reprint Münster 2013; *Elisabeth Schüssler Fiorenza*, Grenzen überschreiten: der theoretische Anspruch feministischer Theologie, Münster 2004; Sabine Demel, Frauen und kirchliches Amt, Vom Ende eines Tabus in der katholischen Kirche, Freiburg i. Br. 2004, followed by an updated version: Frauen und kirchliches Amt, Grundlagen – Grenzen – Möglichkeiten, Freiburg/Basel/Vienna 2012; *Ida Raming*, Gleichrangig in Christus anstatt: Ausschluss von Frauen "im Namen Gottes", Zur Rezeption und Interpretation von Gal 3,27 f. in vatikanischen Dokumenten, Berlin 2006; *Monika Egger/Livia Meier/Katja Wissmiller* (eds), WoMan in Church, Kirche und Amt im Kontext der Geschlechterfrage, Berlin 2006; *Iris Müller/Ida Raming*, Unser Leben im Einsatz für Menschenrechte der Frauen in der römisch-katholischen Kirche: Lebensberichte – Hintergründe – Dokumente – Ausblick, Berlin 2007; *Ida Raming/Iris Müller*, "Contra Legem" – a

of the role of women in the religious sphere is breaking down.[67] The lack of consensus is also a legal criterion and may be considered in a balance of interests. Namely, a lack of clarity in the weighting of the different positions can play a role in judging the cogency of arguments. The greater the diversity of opinion on whether the non-admission of women to leading spiritual offices constitutes one of the foundations of a religious community, the weaker the arguments in favour of non-admission exclusively on grounds of gender become.

Another significant criterion is ambiguities and contradictions in one party's conduct. The case of priests in the Anglican Church may serve to illustrate this.

In England the Anglican Church introduced the ordination of female priests in 1994. Thereupon a number of Anglican clergy left the Anglican Church to join the Roman Catholic Church. One problem concerned converts who were married and wished to continue to serve as parish priests. These former Anglican priests were not celibate, a prerequisite for the Catholic priesthood. The Pope granted about 200 applicants a dispensation, allowing them, although married, to be ordained as Roman Catholic priests.[68] The Anglican priests' conversion was primarily a protest against the acceptance by the Anglican Church of gender equality in the priesthood. They were rewarded for their problematic motivation with ordination in the Roman Catholic Church without a commitment to celibacy, although the Catholic Church continues to refuse its own female theologians admission to the priesthood. Thanks to this dispensation there are now married Roman Catholic priests. Not only Roman Catholic female theologians are dissatisfied with this preferential treatment, but also many Catholic priests, who find the distinctions in treatment regarding the prohibition of marriage troublesome when they themselves have difficulties with the vow of celibacy.

matter of conscience, Our lifelong struggle for human rights for women in the Roman Catholic Church, Berlin 2010; *Doris Strahm* (ed.), Rabbinerinnen, Kantorinnen, Imaminnen, Muftis, Pfarrerinnen, Bischöfinnen, Kirchenrätinnen, Leitungsfunktionen von Frauen im Judentum, im Christentum und im Islam, Basel 2011.

67 This development is not restricted to so-called western cultural circles. It is taking place – at different speeds – in all parts of the world; for Islam see *Amirpur*, pp. 34 ff.; 131 ff., 158 ff. and *Manea*, passim; for Judaism *Greenspahn*, pp. 245 ff.; *Wallach-Faller*, pp. 59 ff.

68 *Theologische Realenzyklopädie*, vol. 36, parts 4–6, pp. 734, ll. 39 ff.

Chapter 2 Priesthood only for men as an expression of religious freedom – or: What is a conflict of fundamental rights?

A conflict of fundamental rights between private or non-state parties requires mediation by a state institution. A conflict of fundamental rights exists if one party's appeal to a fundamental right simultaneously affects a sphere of the counterparty that is protected as a fundamental right. Distinctive features of conflicts of fundamental rights in the religious sphere include: inequality of power between the opposing parties, the argument of leaving the Church and the "Tendenzbetrieb" argument. The fundamental rights of the adversely affected party are to be accorded greater weight if the interfering party renders it totally impossible for the adversely affected party to exercise his fundamental rights.

2.1. Conflict of fundamental rights and the exercise of fundamental rights

In conflicts of fundamental rights between private actors the state functions as mediator, provided that the constellation contains grounds for settlement in a court of law. Therefore, a case of conflict must accord with the pattern of a three-way relationship in which the state has an interest in mediating in the dispute between the interfering party and victim.

Numerous situations are conceivable in which the state has an interest in cases involving fundamental rights. The state has an interest, for instance, when religious communities are recognised (by the state) under public law.[69] The associated special rights (enhanced status, tax-raising powers, right to give religious instruction in state schools, pastoral workers' access to prisons, hospitals, etc.) are combined with a greater duty of compliance with fundamental rights. In particular, the religious communities recognised under public law must take the fundamental rights of their own adherents seriously.[70]

69 See *Hafner*, Religionsfreiheit, pp. 145 ff.; *Hafner*, Kirchen, pp. 330 ff.

70 *Hafner*, Religionsfreiheit, p. 145.

The state also has an interest when parish employees are (co-)financed by public bodies, namely the cantons[71] or when the state undertakes to provide university education for the clergy, which as a rule includes establishing and financing theological faculties. Despite the fundamental separation of church and state, state co-financing of religious communities (subsidies for church personnel, ecclesiastical universities, institutions run by religious communities such as kindergartens, maintenance of church buildings and other sacred buildings) is permissible and in practice widespread.[72]

The state also has an interest when the organisational structures of churches and religious communities recognised by the competent public authority are modelled on the public law system.[73]

If the state has an interest in a conflict between the fundamental rights of the actors involved (a religious community and a private individual), then a triangle in the aforementioned sense exists. Finally, it needs to be established whether a conflict of fundamental rights exists. This is the case if both parties to the conflict have constitutionally protected positions. Thus, on the one hand an act of interference itself has to enjoy constitutional protection (priesthood only for men as an expression of religious freedom). On the other the act of interference must violate a constitutionally protected sphere of the victim (non-discriminatory admission to a spiritual office as an expression of equality). Only then does the state have a duty to find a balance. In the conflict between the constitutional rights of equality and of (corporative) religious freedom the religious community – by claiming its constitutional freedoms – at the same time interferes with the exercise of constitutional rights by the other party (the woman affected by a discriminatory religious practice).

The right of a religious community to define the criteria for a spiritual office can reasonably be viewed as exercising (corporative) religious freedom. To this extent, the act of infringement (defining admission to offices in a way that excludes women) is initially to be regarded as an expression of religious freedom. The argument that a discriminatory definition of the criteria for a spiritual office does not promote a legitimate objective[74] will be examined in the discussion on weighing up competing interests.[75]

---

71 For instance, in the Canton of Berne (Art. 19 para. 1 Law on the Cantonal Churches of Berne) and in the Canton of Basel-Landschaft (§§ 8 ff. Law on the Cantonal Churches).

72 Compared to Switzerland, state subsidies for churches are even higher in Germany, see *Frerk*, passim. For a good overview of legal relations between state and churches in the Federal Republic of Germany see *Brosi*, pp. 219 ff. (edited by *Irina Kreusch*).

73 On the terminology of the corporations of public law in the religious sphere see *Hafner*, Kirchen, pp. 295 ff.; *Krauss*, pp. 7 ff.; *Brosi*, pp. 267 ff.

74 See *Freivogel*, Art. 3 note 28.

75 See chap. 4.3.2.

The counterparty also has to have a constitutionally protected sphere. Even if canon law does not provide for a legal right to priesthood, the absolute non-admission of women to the office is a gender-based discrimination that contradicts the nationally and internationally codified right to gender equality.[76]

Thus, by asserting its corporative religious freedom to ensure its right to define the criteria for admission to spiritual offices, and by formulating its definition in a way that is not gender-neutral, the religious community violates the right to equality of its female members. The state court has the duty to judge the violation in accordance with the principles of the rule of law, i.e., to explore how to resolve the conflict of interests between the two equally protected constitutional rights. This is the context in which the competing interests are weighed up so as to resolve the contradiction in the specific legal case.

2.2. Weighing up competing interests

Cases of conflicts of fundamental rights in the religious sphere need to take certain distinctive features into account. As a rule, there is an *imbalance of power* between the adversaries. Compared to an individual affected by discrimination, religious communities are real power centres.[77] Elements of this power position include the powerful institutional infrastructure of the religious community, but also its authoritative social status. In addition, a precondition and simultaneously a consequence of these power factors is its cumulative authoritative self-image in its dealings with the outside world as well as with its own community members. The result is an imbalance of power between the parties in issues of equality, independent of whether non-admission to offices affects only one specific person or a number of people in the same position. In general the religious community acts as a uniform entity and is also perceived as such by third parties. In contrast, regardless of number, the individual women affected by the discriminatory practice are significantly less prominent and dominant. This is also a consequence of the fact that the perception of inequality as a relevant element of discrimination is a relatively recent development. This starting point is unfavourable for one side and needs to be taken into account in weighing up competing interests.

Another feature is the *issue of avoidance*. Can the discriminated party avoid the conflict of fundamental rights by leaving the community? A priori, i.e., before considering the consequences, the answer is yes.

Avoidance by leaving is also a favoured response to those who reject the argument that an organisation serves specific ideological or spiritual ends (*Tendenzbetrieb*). In this view, religious communities are institutions with a certain substan-

[76] *Ahlers*, pp. 7 ff.

[77] *Hafner*, Religionsfreiheit, p. 144; *Traitler*, pp. 59 f.

tive orientation. Whoever joins and belongs to the religious community approves of its ideological orientation. An individual who disagrees with the community's orientation can leave the community at any time.

However, the option of leaving the religious community may place affected members in an unreasonable *either-or situation*. Leaving also means renouncing one's existing status as a member of the community. For female theologians of the corresponding religious community leaving has, as a rule, serious consequences for their professional career and hence their livelihood. Therefore, within the scope of weighing up competing interests the question arises of whether, to escape the discriminatory attitude of a faith community, a female member of that religious community can be expected to turn her back on it.

In 1984, the European Commission of Human Rights (now the European Court of Human Rights) reached the following decision about the Jewish divorce document (*ghet*):[78] sanctions by the state (e.g. fines) to induce a Jewish husband to present a ghet to his wife would not violate the freedom of religion. According to Jewish religious law (*halacha*), only the husband can apply for divorce and present the ghet.[79] *Sullivan* points out that in this case the state legal system (civil divorce) is not an alternative if cultural conventions and economic dependence oblige women to remain in their original religious community. Even though many of these women wished to lead a life independent of their traditional religious community, these considerations prevented them from doing so.[80]

According to more recent decisions of the Swiss Federal Supreme Court, an either-or situation is not admissible in conflicts of fundamental rights in the religious sphere either. In 2007 the Court approved the right to leave just one part of the Church. A member wanted to leave the Catholic community of Lucerne, but remain a member of the Roman Catholic Church. The Federal Supreme Court ruled that this "partly leaving" the Church was permissible.[81]

2.3. Situations of risk and conflict in the area of fundamental rights

The legislator has a duty to protect fundamental rights from serious challenge by third parties. In Swiss law, for example, this follows from provisions in the Swiss

---

78 D. v. France, App. No. 10180/82, 35 Eur. Comm'n H.R. Dec. & Rep. 199, 202 (1984); HUDOC, Human Rights DOCumentation, http://hudoc.echr.coe.int/, accessed 4 October 2016.

79 *Kröni*, pp. 127 ff.

80 *Sullivan*, p. 847.

81 Swiss Federal Supreme Court (FSC) 134 I 75. With this ruling the Federal Supreme Court changed its view: in 2002 it refused a plaintiff the right to leave one part of the church (see FSC 129 I 68). The change of practice was confirmed in a decision of 9 July 2012 (FSC 2C_406/2011, http://www.bger.ch/index/juridiction/jurisdiction-inherit-template/jurisdiction-recht/jurisdiction-recht-urteile2000.htm, accessed 4 October 2016).

Federal Constitution (SFC) governing the implementation of fundamental rights. In this regard the following provisions of the SFC are crucial:

"Fundamental rights must be upheld throughout the legal system" (Art. 35 para. 1 SFC) and "The authorities shall ensure that fundamental rights, where appropriate, apply to relationships among private individuals" (Art. 35 para. 3 SFC). At the same time, the rights of the counterparty (the interfering party) may be restricted only to the extent that this is justified: "Restrictions on fundamental rights must be justified in the public interest or for the protection of the fundamental rights of others" (Art. 36 para. 2 SFC). This raises the question of weighing up competing interests with a view to achieving a balance between the opposing parties to ensure that the fundamental rights of one party are not accorded undue priority.

Accordingly, in the case of conflicts not only the court, which has the duty to apply the law, but the legislator, too, is called upon to act. The latter has a duty to prevent such conflicts in the individual case by anticipating them already at the legislative level. Accordingly, the legislator should forestall situations in which a challenge to or conflict over fundamental rights may arise by anticipating them at the legislative level and putting safeguards in place. In this respect, the legislator has a relatively free hand, as it does in deciding how broadly these protective measures should be defined. However, if significant legal interests are severely affected, the legislator must take corresponding, effective measures.[82] In the EU and Switzerland the laws passed to protect gender equality relate primarily to the field of employment. The Swiss law on gender equality,[83] for instance, deals primarily with equality in employment. The most important international convention to protect woman, the CEDAW, has a wider remit, however. Besides specific laws and other state institutions that discriminate against women, it also seeks to combat discrimination by non-state actors, in particular discriminatory traditions, practices and patterns.[84]

---

82 *Martin*, p. 133.

83 Federal Act on Gender Equality (SR 151.1).

84 See for instance Arts. 2 (f) and 5 (a) *Convention on the Elimination of All Forms of Discrimination against Women* (CEDAW) (highlighting by the author).
Article 2
States Parties condemn discrimination against women in all its forms, agree to pursue by all appropriate means and without delay a policy of eliminating discrimination against women and, to this end, undertake:
(e) To take all appropriate measures to eliminate discrimination against women by any *person, organization or enterprise*;
(f) To take all appropriate measures, including legislation, to modify or abolish existing laws, regulations, *customs and practices* which constitute discrimination against women;
Article 5
States Parties shall take all appropriate measures:

In areas outside of employment the legislator has shown a degree of inertia, even though the legislator is bound by the CEDAW and the provisions of the Swiss constitution[85] to enact protection laws. In addition, the protection law has the advantage of regulating in one and the same law infringements against the fundamental rights of the interfering party. For, any restriction of the fundamental rights of the interfering party must also have a legal basis.

By leaving the resolution of conflicts of fundamental rights to the courts, the legislator forces the courts to rule on complex situations. Whereas the legislator, however, has to formulate a protection law with universal validity, the court's duty of evaluation is focused on one specific case alone. Even if the court's ruling affects future cases, the court's starting point is from the outset more clearly defined than that of (general and abstract) legislation. Nevertheless, the court's duty to rule on discriminatory practices of religious communities in respect of admission to spiritual offices is a challenging task.

The focus on the individual case also impacts the scope of a court's decision. What happens if, in a case of a conflict of fundamental rights between gender equality and the (corporative) religious freedom of a religious community or church, the court concludes that it is necessary to infringe on the fundamental rights of the party preventing gender equality (the interfering party)? In case study 1 a court would possibly reach the following conclusion: the theological faculty has a legal duty to train male and female theologians, but not to decide whether a prospective female theology student is to be admitted to a seminary (because that is the responsibility of the seminary authorities). Moreover, the court could conclude that if it is the intention to widen the faculty's competence to include decisions on admission to the seminary, its legal mandate must be expanded accordingly. However, the amendment must be formulated in such a way that it satisfies the principle of gender equality.

Such a decision opens up several courses of action for the losing parties. If the current practice of limiting admission to the seminary, which applies strictly to students, is maintained, to the extent that the criteria for admission discriminate on the grounds of gender, the theological faculty must refrain from active involvement in decisions on seminary applications. The seminary must resolve the issue on its own. This in turn may trigger certain dynamics within the religious community that, in the ideal case, will lead to new (satisfactory) solutions for the original issue. It is conceivable that the seminary authorities in collaboration with the fac-

(a) To modify the *social and cultural patterns of conduct* of men and women, with a view to achieving the elimination of prejudices and customary and all other practices which are based on the idea of the inferiority or superiority of either of the sexes or on *stereotyped roles* for men and women.

85 See, among others, Art. 2 CEDAW and Art. 8 para. 3 SFC.

ulty revise their practice concerning the admission of female theology students without creating a separate department for lay theologians (men and women). In this way the seminary would take account of the court's judgement on a specific discriminatory practice (non-admission of the female theology student to the seminary) alone. Even though this does not resolve the principle of ordination to the priesthood, intermediate steps (opening up the seminary) can trigger other developments.

The quality of a court ruling depends materially on a comprehensive summary of the documents used to establish the facts. In court proceedings on the question of priority between equality and religious freedom this also includes the analysis of various doctrines and opinions on the dispute and the careful processing of scholarly literature. The court must thoroughly acquaint itself with the particular characteristics of the diverging positions and study the different points of view in detail. This is an expression of procedural justice.[86] Furthermore, in resolving a conflict of fundamental rights none of the fundamental legal interests involved "may be realised in full at the expense of the opposing interests".[87]

The search for the most considerate balance in a conflict of fundamental rights necessitates a processual approach. The resolution of the balance of interests lies in approximating an optimum. This is particularly evident with a fundamental right such as the principle of equality, which is fundamentally inaccessible to restriction because in the last instance every qualification results in inequality.[88]

A court ruling in case study 1 hardly obliges the seminary (which is not involved in the proceedings at all) to admit the prospective theology student on the ground of gender neutrality. The court could decide that the letter of rejection from the theological faculty constitutes a violation of the principle of gender equality. If it deems the rejection to be inadmissible, the losing party must find a solution that takes into account the female theology student's right to gender equality. The seminary could create a setting that allows female students of theology to complete their studies within the framework of communal values and living offered by a seminary. Moreover, the faculty and seminary authorities are free to move in a direction that allows them to work within the universal church to change attitudes towards the gender question.[89]

If tradition or the appeal to God's eternal plan prevents or complicates admission to the highest spiritual offices[90] this does not only constitute a measurable

86 See also the concept in American law of structural due process in *Martin*, p. 196; *Schefer* p. 81.

87 *Martin*, p. 229.

88 *Hafner*, Religionsfreiheit, p. 152.

89 That said, the solution may not be limited to simply creating a separate lay department in the seminary.

90 See the history of women in the rabbinate in Judaism, *Nadell*, pp. 155 ff.

inequality for women. Inequality based solely on gender impedes the development of women insofar as they internalise their second-class status.[91] In a modern state under the rule of law the implementation of national and international standards of fundamental rights emphasises the dignity of the individual, which includes people's right to develop their individual potential. Conflicts with other fundamental rights that arise from the women's right to gender equality cannot be left unattended. A properly considered process must reconcile them with a view of humans that embraces gender equality. The fundamental rights of the impaired party must be assigned greater weight whenever the interfering party renders the other party's exercise of fundamental rights "completely impossible".[92] Applied to the issue of admission to leading spiritual offices, this strengthens the position of the women who have – de facto or de jure – been refused admission.

91 *Nadell* describes this feeling of second-class status among American Jewish female students who feel socialised as feminists on the university campus, but on the Sabbath find themselves back in their second-class status as women (*Nadell*, p. 161).

92 *Martin*, p. 251.

Chapter 3 Practical concordance, or: Resolving the conflict between gender equality and religious freedom

Overview of arguments and counterarguments. Lack of equal rights in other world religions? Issue of admission to religious offices is on the agenda in almost all religious communities. An emerging new consensus on the admission of women to leading spiritual offices. Schism argument. Termination of the liturgical ceremony because ordained parish leaders have been replaced by authorised (non-ordained) parish leaders. Arguments for tradition become counterproductive inasmuch as insistence on traditional roles jeopardises precisely these traditions.

3.1. Admission to leading offices in other world religions

Occasionally, efforts to defuse the issue of priesthood for women in the Roman Catholic Church refer to the comparable status of women in Judaism and Islam. It is argued that women are not freely admitted to the Jewish rabbinate or leading offices in Islam either. Highlighting an equality of inequality, however, does not justify the discrimination practised in the first instance.

Furthermore, in contrast to the ordained ministries in the Roman Catholic Church, absolute exclusion is unknown in Judaism and Islam, even though in quantitative terms the number of women in leading offices in these religions is still small. In Judaism Orthodox congregations cite a medieval religious law to justify the exclusion of women from the rabbinate.[93] In particular the Reform movement in Judaism takes the view that neither theology nor religious law provides fundamental grounds for prohibiting the female rabbinate. Modern Orthodox congregations, too, also accept that there is some scope in this regard. Despite this, in practice very few women serve as rabbis.[94]

The primary sources in Islam, the Qu'ran and the hadiths, do not contain any verses that can be used to justify a fundamental prohibition of women from spiritual offices. Theoretically, leading offices such as those of mufti, legal scholar or

---

93 *Strahm*, p. 94.

94 In Switzerland there is only one woman serving as a rabbi; see the interview with Bea Wyler in the interview section.

religious judge are open to them, although traditional social roles militate against this in practice. In principle, woman may work as imams.[95] That said, it would be frowned upon for a woman to preside at a mixed-gender prayer meeting, if not prohibited outright.[96]

The primary reason given by the Roman Catholic Church for not admitting women to the priesthood is the gender of the founder and the long, undisputed tradition of male priesthood.[97] This argument was detailed in the Declaration *Inter Insigniores* and confirmed by the Pope in 1994, when the mandatory nature was underscored by the statement: "this judgment is to be definitively held by all the Church's faithful".[98]

In 1976 the Pontifical Biblical Commission emphasised in a report still kept under lock and key[99] that in the New Testament "there are no manifest impediments to admitting women to the priesthood".[100] During the preparations for the Declaration *Inter Insigniores* the Congregation for the Doctrine of the Faith commissioned its own group of experts – the Pontifical Biblical Commission – to study what the Bible says on the question of the admission of women to the priesthood. Contrary to the expectation of the Congregation for the Doctrine of the Faith, the majority of the Biblical Commission came to the conclusion that the possibility of admitting women to the ministerial priesthood could not be unequivocally and definitively excluded.[101] The Congregation, however, felt that the Commission's conclusion was "not helpful and consigned it to the archives"[102].

---

95 See the interview with Dr Rajaa Naji al Mekkawi in the interview section.

96 See *Strahm*, pp. 61 ff., 92 f.

97 On the concept, see *Ratzinger*, pp. 267 ff.

98 In 1995 in a responsum by the Congregation for the Doctrine of the Faith to the issue of ordination the Pope's doctrinal pronouncement was declared to belong to the deposit of faith, which gives the judgment the status of infallibility (see *Strahm/Rudolf*, p. 38). On the question of infallibility see, however, *Demel*, pp. 81 ff. (see also fn. 169 below).

99 See *Gross*, Bericht, pp. 25 ff.

100 Quoted in *Hünermann*, p. 125. The text of the report of the Pontifical Biblical Commission is printed in *Swidler/Swidler*, pp. 338 ff., where commission and conclusion are formulated as follows (pp. 338 and 346): "The Pontifical Biblical Commission was asked to study the role of women in the Bible in the course of research being carried out to determine the place that can be given to women today in the church. The question for which an answer is especially sought is whether or not women can be ordained to the priestly ministry (especially as ministers of the eucharist and as leaders of the Christian community). (…) It does not seem that the New Testament by itself alone will permit us to settle in a clear way and once and for all the problem of the possible accession of women to the presbyterate."

101 *Gross*, Bericht, p. 25.

102 *Gross*, Bericht, p. 25.

3.2. Theological arguments and the weighing up of competing legal interests

A procedure known as *practical concordance*[103] can be applied in cases of conflict between co-existing, but competing interests in the sphere of fundamental rights. The basis of the procedure is the arguments of the two parties, which are weighed up against each other.

The pros and cons of the argument about the admission of women to the most important religious offices are well documented. This is also partly a reflection of the fact that growing globalisation has helped to make equality and religion omnipresent social topics in the twentieth and twenty-first centuries.

In this regard, the various arguments have already been weighed up in theological circles. The different standpoints and opinions for or against admitting women to leading spiritual offices are documented in the relevant literature. The history and evolution of the various positions are explored and presented within the context of the argument.[104] A court seeking to find a balance between competing interests can refer to these theological analyses and weightings.

For example, in the declaration on the question of admission of women to the ministerial priesthood in the Roman Catholic Church (*Inter Insigniores*, 1976) references to current practice or to voluntary and general agreement with a convention, a custom or an ordinance are used as a theological argument for preserving a tradition. It is maintained that by calling only men to the priestly order the Church remains faithful to the type of ordained ministry willed by Jesus Christ and followed by the Apostles.[105]

The *argument of continuity* is mentioned several times in *Inter Insigniores*.[106]

Jurisprudence, too, recognises the argument of undisputed, established practice. However, the argument remains valid only for as long as the practice referred to can be shown to continue undisputed. For the assumption of continuity to hold, the practice must reflect a current consensus of the parties involved and of the social environment.[107]

---

[103] *Rhinow/Schefer/Uebersax*, note 524. See also chap. 1.5. (fn. 50) above.

[104] There is a huge body of specialised literature on the topic of women's ordination (in the Roman Catholic Church), see the overview in fn. 66 above.

[105] Inter Insignores; for an English version, see http://www.vatican.va/roman_curia/congregations/cfaith/documents/rc_con_cfaith_doc_19761015_inter-insigniores_en.html (accessed 4 October 2016).

[106] See chapters "1. The Church's Constant Tradition" and "4. Permanent Value of the Attitude of Jesus and the Apostles".

[107] FSC 105 V 49, p. 50 (established practice concerning a divorced wife's right to a widow's pension) and FSC 136 II 113, p. 118 (established practice concerning extension of a residence permit after termination of marriage).

The criterion of continuity has to be judged from the viewpoint of the present. However, the social environment has changed fundamentally since the practice of the Congregation for the Doctrine of the Faith of preventing the ordination of women by not admitting them to the priestly ministry was laid down in *Inter Insigniores* (1976). Since then, there has been a paradigm shift in the issue of gender equality between men and women. The original (explicit or implicit) consensus on the non-admission of women to the priesthood has shrunk to the extent that one must now speak of dissent.[108] The nature of the reasons for the breakdown in consensus – not only greater sensitivity towards the issue of gender equality, but also growing indifference to religion – does not alter the fact of the breakdown.

Juxtaposing time-honoured tradition and the current breakdown of consensus on the question of reserving the priesthood to men deprives the continuity argument of much, if not all, of its validity – to the extent that the consensus gives way to dissent. The loss of validity is relevant regardless of the fact that the original practice lasted for centuries, while the period since the breakdown of consensus is measured in decades. In the legal weighing up of the competing interests in the issue of gender equality in religion the argument of a time-honoured practice contrasts with a social development moving in the opposite direction. The re-orientation of the position of women has accelerated since the 1960s at a rate unprecedented in human history.[109] Today, almost all religious communities have to deal with the issue of admitting women to leading spiritual offices. Many Christian Churches now ordain women,[110] for example the Anglican Church in England and the German Lutherans since 1992. Both have also consecrated female bishops.[111] In 1999 the Christ Catholics in Switzerland decided to admit women to the priestly ministry.

The gender discussion concerning the admission of women to leading spiritual offices is also a topic in the theological literature.[112] In this respect, one must mention in particular the academic research into the history of forgotten

---

108 *Beinert*, pp. 64, 66; in some circles this dissent is still not acknowledged, see *Müller*, Weihesakrament, p. 353.

109 In this context this development is also known as second-wave feminism (to distinguish it from the rise of the women's movement before and after World War I).

110 *Beinert*, p. 66; *Jones*, passim.

111 The General Synod of the Church of England approved legislation for the ordination of women as bishops in 2014. The Synod had voted against the proposed legislation in November 2012. However, at the General Synod in November 2013 the proposals for draft legislation passed with a large majority. Outside the Church of England, the mother church of the Anglican Communion, various provinces voted earlier to appoint female bishops.

112 See e.g. *Beinert*, p. 66; *Hünermann*, pp. 83, 95; see also Wolfgang Lienemann's bibliography of 2000: http://www.theology.de/downloads/frauenordination.pdf (accessed 4 October 2016); for another bibliography on women and priesthood (1974 to 2001) see *Raming*, Priesteramt, pp. 61 ff.

women in the history of Christianity. Furthermore, feminist theologians have extensively researched the transformation of early Christianity without offices into a patriarchal official church and the problematic consequences for the position of women in this religion.[113] It became evident to what extent the "notion of the inferiority and ritual impurity of women" had seeped into the laws and regulations of the church polity, thereby cementing the status of women as non-admissible to high liturgical offices.[114]

The matter-of-factness with which leading spiritual offices are reserved to men is increasingly and universally questioned. The general outline of the breakdown of consensus and unanimity on the question of the exclusion of women from religious offices is becoming manifest. This breakdown is accompanied by the emergence of a new consensus that points in the opposite direction, namely towards opening religious offices to women. This discussion is taking place in all major religions, though in each at its own pace[115].

To what extent such a consensus exists in a specific religious community and in a specific part of the world needs to be determined in each specific case. However, this can be done; in other words, it is possible to reach objective conclusions on this point. Thanks to intensive scientific debate in the literature and in theological discourse within the respective religious communities, the degree of consensus is well documented, annotated and commented on. For Roman Catholic Christianity, for example, there is a comprehensive body of expertise that substantiates the (theological) merits of female ordination[116] – in the final analysis the 1976 opinion of the Pontifical Biblical Commission on the issue of female priests anticipated the subsequent discussion in the specialised literature.

3.3. Paradigm shift in the gender debate

Four main arguments are used not only by the Roman Catholic Church, but also by the other major religious communities,[117] Judaism and Islam, to justify or explain obstacles to the admission of women to leading spiritual offices:

– traditional gender roles;

---

[113] See the bibliographical references in fn. 165.

[114] See *Strahm/Rudolf*, p. 35 (with further bibliographical references).

[115] See *Strahm*, p. 95. See also *Rajaa Naji al Makkawi*, Islamische Lehre in Marokko und Frankreich, lecture delivered at the conference on "Islamische Studien in Deutschland" (Islamic Studies in Germany) in Cologne, 13–14 July 2010; published at: http://www.wissenschaftsrat.de/download/archiv/El_Mekkaoui_dt.pdf (accessed 4 October 2016).

[116] See the bibliographical references in fn. 66 and 165.

[117] Universal gender stereotypes and de facto obstacles to women's admission to leadership structures are also present in other religious groupings. Insofar as they use the justifications mentioned here, the considerations below apply to them as well.

– time-honoured (women-excluding) tradition;
– theological grounds ("God's eternal plan") and
– internal religious ordinances from the Middle Ages or even earlier.

Opposing this argumentation is the global social paradigm shift in the gender debate over the past half century. In the legal context there have been two crucial developments: on the one hand the *codification* of the right to gender equality[118] in national constitutions (e.g. for Switzerland: Art. 8 para. 3 SFC),[119] in international law (e.g. CEDAW) and in other legal systems (e.g. EU gender equality law) and, on the other, social upheavals and changes that, in conjunction with normative gender equality law, are representative of the role shifts in the gender issue.

The paradigm shift in gender relations is not limited to questioning conventional roles. Apart from the immediate issue, such processes of change can also "help resolve" other problems. In the light of the declining membership of Jewish congregations, the question of whether Jewish women who have completed their training as rabbis should logically also be admitted to the rabbinate is directly tied up with the continued existence of a Jewish way of life.[120] The Roman Catholic priesthood for women goes beyond a postulate of equality. Owing to the worsening shortage of priests, a situation is emerging in which more and more

[118] The first international source of law is the Universal Declaration of Human Rights, Art. 2 (1) of which expressly prohibits unequal treatment on the basis of gender. The two UN covenants on human rights of 1966 also contain gender-specific provisions. Art. 2 (2) of the International Covenant on Economic, Social and Cultural Rights prohibits discrimination, and Art. 7 (a) (i) regulates equal remuneration for work of equal value. Art. 10 (2) establishes special protection for mothers (paid leave or leave with adequate social security benefits for working mothers). Finally, Art. 25 of the International Covenant on Civil and Political Rights in conjunction with Art. 2 determines that every citizen regardless of sex shall have the right and opportunity to take part in the conduct of public affairs. Art. 26 of the same covenant establishes equal and effective protection without discrimination before the law for both sexes. Another important source of law of international gender equality law is the CEDAW. By accepting the convention the States Parties commit themselves to undertake special measures to eliminate discrimination without delay, to influence social development in the longer term and to eliminate prejudice and practices based on stereotyped roles for men and women. Furthermore, the States Parties undertake to implement appropriate measures to promote equality in the field of employment as well as in other important areas of life. Sources of law in the European context include the Council of Europe and the EU. The most important human rights treaty of the Council of Europe, the European Convention on Human Rights (ECHR), does not contain a general provision for equality between men and women, only a prohibition on discrimination, which can be invoked in conjunction with rights and freedoms recognised in the convention or in the provisions of the protocols amending the convention. Protocol No. 12 of 4 November 2000 to the ECHR secures a general prohibition of discrimination. Gender is the first of the prohibited grounds for discrimination listed in the protocol. Also see *Büchler*, pp. 88 ff.

[119] Art. 8 para. 3 SFC places an obligation on the state to ensure the equality of men and women (see FSC 137 I 305, 317).

[120] See the interview with Bea Wyler in the interview section.

ordained parish leaders (priests) are replaced by *authorised, non-ordained* parish leaders (lay theologians). As this practice gains ground, the traditional liturgical ceremony is celebrated less and less frequently.[121] Hence, the argument of tradition to justify admission to the priesthood is becoming increasingly ambivalent inasmuch as traditions such as the liturgical ceremony (Eucharist) in particular can no longer be maintained.

In the legal context the argument of *appealing to the consequences*, also has to be considered. Does the implementation of the principle of equality in the religious sphere have adverse consequences? Does the possibility of female ordination or the de facto opening of leading spiritual offices to women trigger schisms and unpredictable splits within religious communities?

Religious communities that have introduced female ordination have to date not experienced disharmonies and splits that they were unable to cope with.[122] In Judaism, which has three main religious movements,[123] a new Orthodox congregation may be founded if a community of like-minded people decides to work together with a female rabbi. This is not regarded as a schism, but as an expression of Judaism in practice.[124]

As a consequence of growing religious and in particular denominational indifference among large sections of the population and the concomitant decline in membership of traditional religious communities, the question of schism in reaction to female ordination is now viewed differently. It can no longer be taken for granted that the admission of women to leading ministries will create rifts among traditionally-oriented adherents. Rather, a situation appears to be emerging, for instance in the Roman Catholic Church, that can be best described as co-existence between the official Church and its progressively-oriented grassroots, who keep out of each other's way as much as possible.[125] Such (tacit) co-existence in protected areas may be a crucial reason why the issue of (official) admission to offices has been left in a kind of limbo in which both the supporters of the priesthood for men and the growing group in favour of change can reach a *modus vivendi*.

The *schism argument* is also weakened by the fact that, as a rule, traditionally-minded faithful have sufficient alternatives at their disposal, which is relevant to the principle of *proportionality*. Economic pressure on the Churches has already induced them to merge services and close churches. This reorganisation has taken place more or less without protest, partly because of the decline in membership.

---

[121] See *Loretan*, Frauen, pp. 60 f.

[122] *Jensen*, p. 105.

[123] See the glossary to the interview with Bea Wyler.

[124] This is the solution adopted by Bea Wyler, a rabbi in Switzerland, who works with a younger, liberal Jewish group in Basel that exists alongside the Basel Jewish Community (IGB).

[125] On the women's church in Roman Catholic circles see *Strahm/Rudolf*, p. 46.

If women were admitted to the priesthood it should be similarly possible with reasonable organisational effort and expense to arrange for a male priest to lead church services for orthodox Catholics. This argument is a workable alternative to the argument of leaving the Church, the usual reply given to Catholic female theologians who criticise the lack of female priesthood.

The time factor also plays a large role in the legal solution in cases involving competing interests.[126] In its rulings in cases of equality the Swiss Federal Supreme Court, for example, has determined that in the equality issue there has been a shift "in public awareness"[127], and this has to be taken into account. This introduces the dimension of the passage of time, whereby the reasonableness of a specific passage of time has to be taken into consideration. In other words, the actors have to be granted a reasonable period of time to revise a particular practice or a conventional attitude or to amend (outmoded) provisions. In applying the criterion of reasonableness the court itself does not specify what how long the reasonable passage of time should be; rather, in its ruling the court evaluates whether the passage of time at the time of the ruling may be regarded as long enough.[128]

3.4. Initial overview of the arguments

The arguments in favour of the principle of equality can be summarised as follows:

- An emerging new consensus on admitting women to leading spiritual offices is (gradually) superseding the earlier consensus on a theologically or traditionally based male priesthood, or transforming it into dissent.
- The steady decline in membership (which affects basically all religious communities), the growing shortage of priests (which affects the Roman Catholic Church), and the emerging lack of trainee clergymen as a consequence of religious indifference are real threats to the continued existence of religious communities. In the light of this, the traditional arguments become counterproduc-

126 A prime example of consideration of the time factor is a decision of the Federal Supreme Court of 27 November 1990 in which the court determined that women in the Canton of Appenzell Innerrhoden shall enjoy political rights and that this decision enters into effect with the notification of the decision of the Federal Supreme Court (FSC 116 Ia 359). See more recently: FSC 137 I 305, 310.

127 See FSC 116 Ia 359 in the case of introducing cantonal voting rights for women in the Canton of Appenzell Innerrhoden.

128 In the ruling of the Swiss Federal Supreme court in the case of introducing cantonal voting rights for women in the Canton of Appenzell Innerrhoden (FSC 116 Ia 359) this aspect is formulated as follows: "The judge has to make every effort to apply a norm in a manner that reflects as closely as possible the facts and opinions of the case. Thus, he will often abandon a traditional interpretation that was doubtless right at the time the law was established, but in view of the change in circumstances, or only because of the shift in opinions, is no longer viable."

tive inasmuch as precisely the insistence on traditional roles jeopardises tradition.

- Implementing the principle of equality in the religious sphere does not have any adverse consequences. In particular, introducing female ordination or opening leading spiritual offices to women has to date not resulted in schisms in religious communities; traditionally-minded members have reasonable alternatives at their disposal.
- In the time that has passed a solution could have been found that would have satisfied all sides.

These four arguments do not exist in isolation. Rather, they are part of a sociological context in which the signs point to a re-orientation in gender roles. A prime aspect of this re-orientation is the increasing acceptance that individuals should determine their own development on the basis of personal potential and choice, independently of imprinted gender roles. This means the above-mentioned arguments are in line with present-day social developments, which makes them more persuasive.

On the other hand contradictions between religious and secular approaches can create a dilemma for members of religious communities.[129] Members of the Roman Catholic Church may be particularly affected, for instance, if some aspects of official statements of the Roman Catholic Church reflect extreme positions that are obviously contrary to social developments. Three factors can serve to deepen this dilemma:

- The Church does not plausibly explain its position; there is the view, for example, that "the theological rationale that only a man can represent Jesus Christ in the priesthood is an *idolatry* of the manhood of Jesus, as this treats his biological maleness as the essence of his being Christ".[130] Given the background of sexual abuse cases, together with the secret practice and public condemnation of homosexuality, these positions leave behind an unpleasant aftertaste.
- No effort is made to develop an approach that can help an individual to solve the dilemma of being both a member of the religious community and a private individual in the secular sphere.
- The Church's positions lead to absurd conclusions (the emancipation of women is not in keeping with God's will).

---

[129] *Hafner*, Spannungsfeld, p. 36.

[130] *Strahm/Rudolf*, p. 45.

Chapter 4 Three case studies of the Roman Catholic Church

Case study 1: (Non-)admission of a female theology student to a seminary? Case study 2: (No) equal remuneration between a parish administrator and a parish priest working as a team? Case study 3: Invalid re-election of a female parish administrator who after many years in office was ordained a priest contra legem?

4.1. Case study 1: Non-admission to the seminary

4.1.1. Background

There are four Roman Catholic faculties of theology in Switzerland:[131] one each at the Universities of Fribourg[132] and Lucerne[133], the private, church-run Chur University of Theology[134] and the newest, the theological faculty of Lugano (Facoltà di Teologia di Lugano),[135] which was founded in 1993.

---

[131] See *Kraus*, Staatskirchenrecht, pp. 352 ff.

[132] The faculty is a state faculty recognised by the Catholic Church under canon law and is subject to canon and state law (on the history of the faculty see Kraus, Staatskirchenrecht, p. 854, fn. 822). An agreement between church and state ensures the participatory rights of the church: Agreement on the Theological Faculty of the University of Fribourg of 8 July 1985 (published on: http://www.lexfind.ch, heading: "Abkommen betreffend die Theologische Fakultät der Universität Freiburg", accessed 8 October 2016).

[133] On the history of the faculty see *Kraus*, Staatskirchenrecht, p. 355, fn. 823. The relationship between church and state concerning the Theological Faculty of the University of Lucerne is regulated in an agreement with the Bishop of Basel: see § 10 para. 1, University Law of the Canton of Lucerne (http://www.lexfind.ch/dta/23942/2/539.pdf, accessed 8 October 2016).

[134] On the history and current status of the Chur University of Theology see *Kraus*, Staatskirchenrecht, p. 355, fn. 824. On state recognition of the university's degrees see the Ordinance on State Recognition of University Degrees and the Organisation of Classes at the Chur University of Theology (SG 427.700, published at http://www.lexfind.ch/dta/23673/2/, accessed 8 October 2016). The Canton of Graubünden pays annual contributions of 300,000 Swiss francs to the Chur University of Theology (see www.dfg.gr.ch [heading: "Dokumentation", "Budget 2016"], accessed 8 October 2016).

[135] According to cantonal church law, state recognition of the Catholic Church of the Canton of Ticino includes church institutions and establishments and, therefore, the faculty of theology; see Art. 1 Legge sulla chiesa (Church Act, Canton of Ticino, http://www.lexfind.ch/dtah/9932

The issue of fundamental rights raised by this case study deal with the conflict between the female theology student's right to gender equality on the one hand and the church's invocation of its religious freedom to reserve training for the priesthood and admission to the seminary to male candidates on the other.[136] In this case study the (fictitious) theological faculty represents the (similarly fictitious) seminary. As the faculty is regulated by cantonal law, the letter of rejection from the faculty is in principle a refusal order;[137] it has to be issued in this form to enable the recipient to request a judicial review of the letter of rejection.

The inclusion of the faculty in the case by this means may appear to be a legal construction; it is, however, intended to illustrate how the case is to be judged from a legal point of view. Other possible constellations could also bring a state court to rule on the non-admission of a female theology student to training for the priesthood.

It would, for instance, be possible to make admission of female students to training a condition for (state) subsidies for a seminary. An agreement of this nature under public law could also be the subject of legal proceedings.

Another course would be to pass a (cantonal) education act that explicitly states that all state and private training courses must be open to both genders. This could open the door for a legal ruling if a seminary were to challenge such a law as a violation of the freedom of religion.

The state can also act in the case of private theological colleges that are recognised under public law if they fulfil certain conditions. As a rule, recognition of degrees and the courses offered by private universities and colleges are regulated by law.[138] Within this framework state legislation could conceivably lay down conditions that require the third party (the church) to make concessions in respect of gender equality. Such provisions could in turn be the subject of judicial complaint proceedings in which the confessional plaintiff invokes its freedom of religion.

1/4/02_35.htm, accessed 8 October 2016; see also the website of the faculty (http://www.teologialugano.ch, accessed 8 October 2016).

136 This case study considers in depth the legal conflict between the fundamental rights of equality and of freedom of religion. In practice the rules for admission to seminaries vary: not all seminaries refuse admission to female theological students. Some seminaries have more liberal admission policies. According to the website of the St Beat Seminary in Lucerne the seminary is the place of residence of candidates for the priesthood during their studies. It states: "Female and male students who intend to enter the service of the diocese as pastoral administrators shall undertake to live in St Beat Seminary for a reasonable period of time during their studies." (See http://www.bistum-basel.ch/de/Bistum/Priesterseminar/Studienbegleitung.html [heading "Richtlinien für die Theologiestudierenden"], accessed 8 October 2016).

137 *Häfelin/Müller/Uhlmann,* note 886.

138 See e.g. the above-mentioned Regulation on the Recognition of University Degrees and the Organisation of Classes at Chur University of Theology (fn. 134).

In the following discussion of the problem of fundamental rights of the (fictitious) case study the female theology student's right to equal treatment conflicts with the church's invocation of its religious freedom to admit only male candidates to training for the priesthood and to the seminary.

4.1.2. *Weighing up competing interests*

To date no court has been asked to rule in a case involving these competing interests.[139] The weighing up of competing interests has not been thoroughly discussed in the academic literature either. It is accepted in principle that in a case that seeks to balance competing interests the freedom of religion or a religious community's right to self-determination should be accorded significant weight.[140]

If an institutional body claims corporative religious freedom or the right to self-determination, the question arises of how to assess the range of opinion within this institution. How should differences of opinion that have emerged in the course of time between the leaders of the religious community and most or all of its members be assessed? Do such discrepancies influence the invocation of the right to self-determination or corporative religious freedom?

The concept of corporative religious freedom and the right to self-determination initially (more or less tacitly) assume that the fundamental right has been invoked by an institution with religious views that are more or less unchallenged. If, however, no unanimous opinion exists (any longer) within the institution that holds the fundamental right and invokes corporative religious freedom or the right to self-determination, or if the views of the leaders deviate substantially from those of most or all of the members, the question then arises of how to assess this situation of dissent when weighing up the competing interests of religious freedom and the principle of equality.

The competence to define who in the institution exercises the right to self-determination may itself be an element of the right to self-determination. There can be no doubt that recognition of corporative religious freedom or the right to self-determination also includes recognition of the right of the institution holding the fundamental right (in this case the Roman Catholic Church) to determine the content that it regards as indispensable for its religion.

The comprehensive right to gender equality at the national and international levels was recognised for the first time in the twentieth century. Accordingly, the

---

139 In Equal Employment Opportunity Commission v. Catholic University of America, 83 F.3d 455 (Court of Appeals, District of Columbia Circuit, 1996) the interests of the parties were not weighed up. For criticism of the decision see *Sunstein*, pp. 367 ff.

140 *Ahlers*, p. 170; *Buser/Loretan*, p. 29; *Buser*, p. 65; *Hafner*, Religionsfreiheit, pp. 152 ff.; *Loretan*, vol. 1, pp. 219 f.; *Wyttenbach*, pp. 406 ff.; see also Eidgenössische Kommission für Frauenfragen (Swiss Federal Commission for Women's Issues), p. 13.

conflict of fundamental rights between religious freedom and gender equality has only relatively recently been acknowledged as a problem. In the meantime, the issue of gender equality has become a reality in all areas of life, whereby the religious sphere has tended to give priority to more defensive positions. However, in most religious communities[141] the debate is now about how to align the status of women with that of men within the religious community. This debate highlights the diversity of views about admitting women to leading religious offices and the gradual breakdown of attitudes that previously took male leadership for granted.

Such prerequisites must be considered in any weighing up of the competing interests between the right to self-determination and the principle of gender equality. The question of who (within the institution) can invoke corporative religious freedom or the right to self-determination is linked to the question of who determines the contents that qua religious freedom or the right to self-determination can be asserted against conflicting positions. If differences (and very possibly controversial ones) are manifest within the institution, this pluralism must be included in the weighing up of the competing interests. In the meantime, dissent over the issue of gender-neutral admission to all offices has become very vocal and must, therefore, be taken into account in weighing up the arguments (the "dissent factor"), especially when the differences of opinion refer to a specific conflict of fundamental rights. If the lack of admission to training induces a female Roman Catholic theology student to invoke her fundamental right of gender equality, then in weighing up the competing interests between gender equality and religious freedom the internal Roman Catholic divergence in the women's issue must be taken into account when weighting the arguments.

The more disparate this divergence, the greater the weight it should be given in weighing up the competing interests. Moreover, if the opinion that diverges from that of the official church exhibits a degree of plausibility on account of, say, its correspondence with a parallel social development, this congruence may strengthen the right to equality at the expense of the right to self-determination.

Finally, the scope of the specific case must not be ignored. The issue in case study 1 initially concerns only whether the female theology student can be admitted to the specific training for the priesthood and to the seminary. Hence, the right to self-determination is claimed solely with reference to these questions of admission. A positive ruling (that recognises the right of the theology student) would not prejudice the issue of female priests, especially as the training for the priesthood alone does not create a legal claim to ordination. In this situation the

---

[141] See the interviews with Dr Ida Raming, Rabbi Bea Wyler and Rajaa Naji al Makkawi PhD in the interview section.

right to self-determination would not be subject to severe, but only to a medium impairment.

The female theology student's request affects only a preliminary stage of the female priesthood, namely admission to the special training for the priesthood. To this extent, the medium degree of impairment of the religious community's right to self-determination must be compared with an equality issue that has been determined to be significant, and one that a growing number of community members also recognise as justified.

The theological publications that substantiate the theological merits of a female priesthood in the Roman Catholic Church are academic studies. They are widely recognised; they fulfil scientific standards and are written mainly by academic staff in theological faculties, or are at least read by them.[142] This academic literature also deals expressly with the arguments of the official church *against* the female priesthood.

Furthermore, the significance of the student's application goes beyond the individual. Besides its effect on the individual, the issue must also be seen in a contemporary social context that favours human behaviour which recognises an individual's rights and options regardless of gender. It is not the intention of the legal action to place restrictions on the church's right to self-determination for the benefit of one individual. Rather, the specific individual case serves as a reference to the collective constellation of inequality (*all* female theology students are excluded from training for the priesthood).

A weighing up of competing interests would also include other arguments. Not only the ongoing paradigm shift in gender roles worldwide favours compliance in the religious sphere; the growing shortage of priests is also an argument for admitting female theology students to training for the priesthood. The inconsistence of the traditional understanding of the church's office, which may ultimately result in the loss of traditions (e.g. in the Eucharistic celebration), is to some degree also a qualification of the church's right to self-determination.

In the final instance, the weighing up of competing interests is essentially the question of whether the disadvantages of practising gender equality in admission to training for the priesthood are greater than giving priority to the traditional understanding of church offices. Conversely, the question may be posed as to which offers greater utility: admitting female theology students to training for the priesthood or maintaining the tradition of training only men for the priesthood?

Even if educational institutions for priests were to immediately admit (female and male) lay theologians, this would not be a satisfactory solution. Church employees with a degree in theology point out that they cannot properly identify with

[142] See the review of the literature in fn. 66.

the term lay theologian as it sounds amateurish, which does not do justice to the merits of their professional and idealist commitment.

Some four decades have passed since the issue of female priests emerged and started the on-going academic and theological debate. Gender stereotypes continue to be broken down all over the world. And it is pointed out with growing insistence that both crass and more subtle forms of discrimination against women committed in the name of religious freedom are no longer acceptable.[143]

4.1.3. Summary of the arguments; conclusion

In summary the arguments against the church's right to self-determination in respect of the issue of the admission of female theology students to seminaries – on the basis of the same aptitude test for male students – are as follows:

- the breakdown in consensus on the subordinate status of women in the Roman Catholic Church;
- the concomitant discrepancy between the church leadership and most of its members;
- international law on gender equality is committed to combatting not only legal discrimination, but also discrimination in practice and stereotypes in the non-state sector;
- the limited scope of the case in question, in which a ruling in favour of equality does not constitute a prejudice with regard to priestly ordination and to this extent is only a medium impairment of the church's right to self-determination;
- the growing shortage of priests, which calls for the admission of female theology students to training for the priesthood;
- the inconsistency in the church's traditional understanding of its office, which ultimately can result in a loss of tradition and in this respect qualify the church's right to self-determination;
- the greater utility for the (like-minded) community if female theology students who wish and feel they have a corresponding vocation are admitted to training for the priesthood;
- the collective dimension of inequality, in that all female theology students are excluded;
- the unsatisfactory distinction between ordained and lay theologians, which devalues the latter;

---

143 Council of Europe, Committee on Equal Opportunities for Women and Men, Doc. 10670 of 16.9.2005, Women and religion in Europe, Report, section II. C. 14 ff. (http://www.assembly.coe.int/nw/xml/XRef/X2H-Xref-ViewHTML.asp?FileID=11127&lang=en, accessed 8 October 2016); Council of Europe, Parliamentary Assembly Resolution 1464, 4.10.2005 (http://www.assembly.coe.int/nw/xml/XRef/Xref-XML2HTML-en.asp?fileid=17372&lang=en, accessed 8 October 2016).

– a growing global awareness that religious freedom cannot justify crass or subtle forms of discrimination against women;
– the numerous theological expert opinions on the acceptability of female ordination and;
– the lack of evidence that a ruling in favour of equality would precipitate schism.

Giving due consideration to these arguments, a court might give *greater weight* to equality of admission to training for the priesthood than to the counterargument on the part of the theological faculty, which seeks to exclude admission of female students.

4.2. Case study 2: Equal remuneration for priest and female parish administrator

4.2.1. Peculiarities of equality of remuneration

For historical reasons there are a number of different financing models used in church employment contracts. In certain Swiss cantons the salaries of church employees are paid by the state.[144] Where church and state are still largely separate, church staff, including parish priests and parish administrators, are paid by the finance departments of the elected cantonal church councils under cantonal public law. Financial demands are met by revenues from church taxes, income from church property and other sources.[145] The individual parishes receive annual contributions to enable them to fulfil their functions. Joint institutions ensure binding, structured cooperation and consultations take place between the elected cantonal church councils and church institutions. The payment of salaries can also be the responsibility of churches organised under private law.[146] As equality of remuneration is internationally codified[147] and in Switzerland is a constitutional right that

[144] See *Hafner*, Trennung, p. 255; see also fn. 71.

[145] See for example § 28 of the constitution of the Roman Catholic Church of the Canton of Basel-Stadt (http://www.rkk-bs.ch/home/Gesetzessammlung?main=T6242HO3&directory=T6242HO3), accessed 8 October 2016).

[146] E.g. the Canton of Neuchâtel, see *Kraus*, Staatskirchenrecht, p. 300.

[147] Equal pay for equal work is internationally codified: Equal Remuneration Convention, No. 100 of the International Labour Organisation (ILO) on equal remuneration for men and women workers for work of equal value (entry into force in Switzerland in 1973). The UN Convention on the Elimination of All Forms of Discrimination against Women includes the right to equal remuneration in Art. 11 (1) (d). The Council of Europe: European Social Charter of 1961; European Economic Community (EEC, subsequently the EC, superseded by the EU): Art. 157 of the Treaty on the Functioning of the European Union (TFEU) and secondary legislation (ex Art. 119 of the EEC Treaty).

can be asserted against both a public and a private employer,[148] the legal status of the employer in case study 2 is not in question. The fundamental right to equal remuneration has a direct third-party effect. It can be invoked not only in a relationship between the state and an individual (vertically), but also between private individuals (horizontally). Because of the direct third-party effect, an action for equal remuneration in case study 2 is perfectly possible. Hence, unlike in the case of a fundamental right with only an indirect third-party effect, there is no need for a further point of reference involving the state.

4.2.2. Weighing up of competing interests anticipated by the law

A further peculiarity of equal remuneration lies in the fact that the weighing up of the competing fundamental rights has already been anticipated by the law. Therefore, in court proceedings there is no need to weigh up competing interests between equality on the one hand and private autonomy or economic freedom (of the employer) on the other. This weighing up has already been decided by the law in favour of equal remuneration. This is based on the notion that the state has to protect remuneration as it is a particularly vulnerable sphere of working life in which the implementation of the principle of equality needs to be as effective as possible.

Therefore, the first step is to determine whether there is a case for equal remuneration. Equal remuneration refers not only to equal pay for equal work, but also equal pay for work of *equal value*. According to the case law and the relevant literature, equal or equivalent work means "*similar* work that is comparable in terms of the type of activity, the physical and/or mental or psychological demands, responsibility and the necessary or beneficial training"[149].

As the two incumbents in case study 2 are of equal rank and the job profile is regarded as two halves of a parish administration that works as a team, their work can be assumed to be comparable in principle. Both the parish administrator and the parish priest are each responsible in equal shares for the administration of the parish. The parish priest attends to those responsibilities that require ordination: Eucharistic liturgy, anointing of the sick and hearing (the rare) individual confessions. The parish administrator compensates for these specific competencies of the parish priest by taking on all duties of outside representation and attending committee meetings of the elected cantonal church councils. For the rest, the two incumbents share the parish administration. Their work can readily be deemed to be physically, mentally and psychologically comparable.

---

[148] Art 8 para. 3SFC: "Men and women have equal rights. The law shall ensure their equality, both in law and in practice, most particularly in the family, in education, and in the workplace. *Men and women have the right to equal pay for work of equal value.*" (Author's emphasis.)

[149] *Bigler-Eggenberger*, note 91; see also *Bigler-Eggenberger/Kägi-Diener*, notes 118 ff.

The remaining legal issue is whether the parish priest's ordination as compared to the lay status of the female parish administrator warrants the treatment of the two activities as unequal or of unequal value to a degree that justifies the difference in remuneration. If so, in the light of the almost identical activities of the female parish administrator and the parish priest the difference in their theological status must be decisive.

Both incumbents have a degree in theology. The pastoral training of male and female lay theologians more or less imitates the training in a seminary or is focused on the specific requirements of parish administration. Thus, they also pass the test of comparability at the level of training and education. Therefore, all in all the work of the parish administrator and that of the parish priest can be regarded as equal or at least of equal value.

Given this background, the ordination of the male parish administrator cannot be regarded as so decisive as to objectively justify a relatively wide difference in remuneration. Accordingly, the parish priest's higher pay grade violates the principle of equality of remuneration.

It should not be forgotten that this procedure creates a dilemma for the court. In a gender-equality case it grants relevance to a status element (ordination) that is not available to women solely on account of their gender. This inconsistency could induce the court to ignore the criterion from the start because of the problematic nature of this discriminatory issue. The result would be the same, especially because if the discriminatory characteristic were omitted a comparison between the two specific activities of the female parish administrator and the parish priest would produce the result that these are two equal or very similar positions which do not justify a wage difference.

However, this second approach would include a statement (by the state) according to which ordination is a discriminatory element that may not be considered in an equal remuneration case. Such a statement on the part of the authorities would not violate the freedom of religion. A religious community does not have a fundamental right that gives it immunity against official statements about discriminatory religious practices.[150]

[150] In 1991, Osho, a meditation movement (formerly the Bhagwan movement), filed a complaint against the German Federal government, which had described the community as "destructive" and as "a youth sect". The German Constitutional Court and the European Court of Human Rights ruled that the statements did not violate religious freedom, insofar as the neutrality of the state in religious and philosophical matters was preserved (see German Constitutional Court, ruling of 26 June 2002-1 BvR 670/91; CASE OF LEELA FÖRDERKREIS E.V. AND OTHERS v. GERMANY; judgment of the Court of Human Rights of 6 November 2008; the decision can be accessed in the Court's database of case-law (HUDOC, Human Rights DOCumentation, http://hudoc.echr.coe.int/, accessed 9 October 2016); see also *Brosi*, p. 229.

In practice, the elected cantonal church councils responsible for salary regulations are intent on ensuring equal remuneration between female theologians and ordained ministers who share administrative responsibilities. On the other hand, discussions about higher salary grades for ordained parish administrators may arise in the preparatory phase of determining the legal basis for remuneration – for instance, if the restructuring of pastoral functions introduces organisational forms that distinguish between *priests with the function of leaders* on the one hand and *female and male lay theologians as extraordinary parish administrators* on the other.

4.3. Case study 3: Re-election of a female priest

4.3.1. Background

Case study 3 concerns the re-election of a parish administrator who, after being elected to a third term in office, was ordained a priest *contra legem*[151] before standing for a fourth term. The following should be noted about the parish election: the democratic parish election, which grants the parish the right to elect its parish priest, is a special case in Switzerland.[152] In certain respects the parish election contradicts the principles of canon law; however, it is regarded as an "acceptable form of appointing a parish priest".[153] Can. 523 CIC states: "Without prejudice to the prescript of can. 682 § 1, the provision of the office of pastor belongs to the diocesan bishop, and indeed by free conferral, unless someone has the right of presentation or election." In terms of the canon law provision, the democratic election of the parish priest is qualified as a right of presentation and election.[154] Since the late Middle Ages parishes have had the right to elect their parish priest. Later, individual cantonal governments claimed the right to elect parish priests, which they transferred to the parishes in the nineteenth century. Parishes exercise the right to elect their parish priest. In certain cases it is used only for the first election of a parish priest. After that, at the end of his four or five-year term of office a parish priest is deemed to be re-elected *in a tacit election* (the only candidate is declared elected without an election being held), unless a predetermined proportion of the eligible voters (e.g. one fifth or 100 eligible voters) in the local

[151] On the term see fn. 38.

[152] See *Kraus*, Staatskirchenrecht, pp. 384 ff. A few cantons do not have a specific cantonal regulation, or the relevant provisions are to be found in the constitutions of the cantonal churches, see *Kraus*, Staatskirchenrecht, p. 384.

[153] See *Kraus*, Staatskirchenrecht, p. 386. On the relationship between the requirement of democracy and the right of the Roman Catholic Church to organise itself, see also *Hafner*, Demokratie, pp. 80 ff.

[154] *Kraus*, Staatskirchenrecht, p. 386.

parish requests a ballot-box vote.[155] However, this does not apply in all cantons. The regulations governing the election of parish priests vary widely.[156] Thus some cantons, for example the Cantons of Zurich and Aargau, require regular elections of parish priests.[157]

Where provision is made for the election of the parish priest, as a rule this also applies to the election of female and male parish administrators.[158]

In case study 3 there is a choice of two procedures for a re-election, a ballot-box election and a tacit election. In the first variant the case study assumes that the parish administrator or female priest *contra legem* is unanimously re-elected. In the second variant, the tacit election, the requisite quorum of eligible voters requests a public election. As a rule, in the case of a tacit election such a request is the consequence of dissatisfaction with the parish priest currently in office. The object of circumventing a tacit election is to prevent the confirmation in office of a parish priest the community does not approve of (or no longer approves of). In case study 3 a ballot-box election is requested for the opposite reason. The public election is intended to express the parish's unanimous acceptance of the female parish administrator. To make matters clear, the following assumption holds for model case 3: the current parish administrator or female priest *contra legem* is unanimously re-elected in a public election.

It is further assumed that the executive of the elected cantonal church council declares the election invalid because, according to canon law, only an ordained minister can be elected as a parish priest. The elected parish administrator and the parish appeal against this ruling of annulment. Both claim that the annulment violates the principle of gender equality and the autonomy of the local authority (i.e. the autonomy of the parish in electing the parish priest).

---

155 See e.g. Art. 26 of the electoral and voting regulations of the Roman Catholic Church Basel-Stadt (electoral code), published on the website of the Roman Catholic Church Basel-Stadt (http://www.rkk-bs.ch/home/Gesetzessammlung?main=T6242HO3&directory=T6242HO3, see "Wahl- und Abstimmungsordnung"; accessed 9 October 2016).

156 On the different cantonal regulations see *Kraus*, Staatskirchenrecht, pp. 383 ff.

157 § 112 para. 2 Constitution of the Canton of Aargau, Art. 24 para. 1 (b) Statute of Organisation of the Roman Catholic Regional Church of the Canton of Aargau, published on the website of the Roman Catholic Church of Aargau (http://www.kathaargau.ch/_download_pdf/Gesetzessammlung/1_Organisationsstatut.pdf, accessed 9 October 2016). In the Canton of Thurgau the law on the organisation of the cantonal catholic church (which corresponds to a cantonal church constitution) is in the process of revision; one proposal is to abolish tacit election in favour of regular re-election.

158 See e.g. Art. 26 of the electoral and voting regulations of the Roman Catholic Church of Basel-Stadt (fn. 155); § 67 (1) and (2) Law on the Organisation of the Roman Catholic Regional Church of the Canton of Thurgau, http://www.lexfind.ch/dtah/97025/2/188.21.pdf, accessed 9 October 2016.

The court could see a point of reference for the state in the public election[159] and in the church council's ruling of annulment. In deciding on the validity of the election the court has to consider the conflict of fundamental rights between gender equality on the one hand and the church's right to self-determination on the other. The church's right to self-determination comes into play through the church council's ruling of annulment, as the church council works on the assumption of the non-admission of women to the priesthood under canon law. The secondary subject of parish autonomy, invoked by the parish affected by the annulment of the election, is ignored in the following.

The court may assume that the election would have been approved if the candidate had stood for election in her functions as parish administrator and lay theologian. Instead, in the re-election she stood as an ordained female priest *contra legem*, which is why the election was annulled. The objection is not to an irregularity in the electoral procedure, but to what the church authorities and the elected cantonal church councils regard as an arrogation of status on the part of the elected female parish administrator.

Against this background, the court is faced with the fundamental problem of how as a state institution that is bound to observe international and national law on gender neutrality it has to deal with the question of gender-discriminatory ordination.

4.3.2. Weighing up the competing interests

The principle of practical concordance used in weighing up competing interests between two opposite positions seeks to find a compromise. However, gender equality can on principle not be qualified as this would then be inequality. This is a peculiarity of the principle of gender equality. If, despite this, one party pursues settlement proceedings through a balance of competing interests, this peculiarity will have to be given due consideration. In such proceedings a qualification of the principle of gender equality may be allowed under very tight constraints, for instance if *exceptionally weighty grounds* can be asserted by the fundamental right in the conflict, i.e. the church's right to self-determination or religious freedom. The weightiness of these grounds may for example be the far-reaching consequences of a court ruling.

If the election in case study 3 were confirmed by a court ruling, the elected cantonal church councils and the church would have to accept the decision because state law has precedence. Notwithstanding this, there is nothing to prevent the church from viewing religious acts of the female priest *contra legem* as invalid

---

[159] See FSC 108 Ia 82 (removal of a parish priest); FSC 108 Ia 264 (unauthorised election of a parish priest).

under canon law. This would primarily affect the actions of the parish administrator pertaining to the Eucharistic liturgy. In principle the activities that she has carried out to date as parish administrator would not be affected. Such a situation would mean that under canon law the parish administrator was performing valid and invalid actions alongside one another. At the same time and in full knowledge of the circumstances, parish members would request or tolerate activities by the parish administrator, although under canon law their validity would be in question or unclear.

The associated dilemma of conscience for the individual member who makes use of such services (e.g. participation in an "unlawful" Eucharistic liturgy) should not be underestimated. Such concerns are, however, limited with respect to both place (the parish in question) and time (e.g. when the parish administrator reaches retirement age). Moreover, they are only possible when there is a relatively broad, stable consensus in the parish, without which the preceding exceptional parish election would not have been conceivable. The scope of a corresponding court ruling is, therefore, restricted to the special individual case. For this reason, the argument of weighty grounds in support of the church's right to self-determination probably does not hold.

The next step is to consider the consensus argument. Currently, when a Roman Catholic female lay theologian performs a funeral Mass, she may read from the Gospel, deliver funeral sermons, remove the ciborium containing the consecrated host from the tabernacle, recite prayers at the altar in front of the chalice and then distribute communion. A public that generally attends church as part of family celebrations and, therefore, with *limited experience* of the liturgy can scarcely distinguish between an ordained priest and the female lay theologian in a white cassock. One possible conclusion is that ordination, therefore, no longer has great significance and that outwardly gender equality has almost been achieved. However, it is not the aim of gender equality to achieve an externally deceptive resemblance. The unequal starting point would be perpetuated, resulting in a precarious equality that could be reversed or restricted at any time. Therefore, the approximation in external appearance is not a ground for restricting the priesthood to men. On the contrary, the acceptance by churchgoers of the similarity in appearance may be taken as further evidence of consensus on admitting women to the priesthood.[160]

In case study 3 consensus of this nature is reflected in the unanimous electoral result. Although democratic unanimity cannot rectify all aspects of invalidity in an election, when the cause of invalidity is solely the "wrong" gender of the elected individual and, therefore, is the consequence of gender discrimination, the unan-

[160] On the question of whether lay ministries also have a "sacramental quality" see *Bausenhart*, pp. 306 ff., 321 ff.

imity of the acting church members may be considered to be an argument of some weight.

A possible infringement of the church's right to self-determination is mitigated inasmuch as a court decision that declares the election to be valid does not answer the question of whether, because of the principle of equality, the Roman Catholic Church must open up the priesthood to women. The infringement is limited to excluding a pre-existing discriminatory element pertaining to the issue of the validity of the re-election of a parish administrator ordained *contra legem*.

It is worth asking whether the issue of the female priesthood should or must be resolved within the framework of weighing up competing interests between the principle of gender equality and the Church's right to self-determination. To date the state has held back from enforcing gender equality legislation in the religious sphere, largely because other spheres of life – employment, politics, business, family and education – required more urgent action to resolve disparities between laws and practices on the one hand and the principle of gender equality on the other. With the passage of time the focus on discrimination in the religious sphere has grown. The question of whether the gender equality law should play a role in appointments to senior spiritual offices[161] can also reformulated: why should the law on gender equality not apply to specific offices in the hierarchical system in the religious sphere? Is there any logical reason why in controversies about the reservation of specific offices exclusively to men in the religious sphere the competing interests between the right to gender equality and the religious community's right to self-determination should not be weighed up? Should the non-admission of women to important spiritual offices not be questioned and the contradiction with the principle of gender equality be accepted?

These questions are also asked by theologians and attempts are made to answer them with theological arguments. The arguments can be found in the extensive academic literature on the theological grounds for the female priesthood. The corresponding investigations are evidence of a growing consensus within the church about (Roman Catholic) female priesthood. The investigations also deal in depth with the church's arguments for restricting ordination to men. Paramount among the church's arguments are the long undisputed tradition of the male priesthood and the biological fact that Jesus and the 12 apostles were male.[162] These arguments have been discussed in great detail in theology and there are ample

---

[161] The role of public courts as "arenas" for religious conflicts has also been explored with respect to other religions: see *Reuter/Kippenberg*, p. 15.

[162] Another argument, though not strongly rooted among the faithful, is the symbolism of the Church as bride and Jesus as bridegroom; for a detailed account see *Müller*, Weihesakrament, pp. 299 ff.

evidence and studies to refute them. The counterarguments of reputable theologians, female and male, may be summarised as follows:

The historical, patriarchal conditionality of the undisputed male tradition,[163] which came about mainly through the expansion of the church as a strictly hierarchical organisation, and also the memory of the connection between manliness and religion in archaic initiation rites and the resulting "idolatry"[164] of maleness, has been thoroughly documented and substantiated. At the same time, it has been shown that evidence of the role of women was consistently and radically erased – for instance the existence of female apostles, deaconesses and women in priestly functions in the early church.[165] On account of the "ground-breaking role"[166] it plays in feminist biblical exegesis, one passage in St Paul's letter to the Galatians is regularly cited: "For all of you who were baptised into Christ have clothed yourselves in Christ. There is neither Jew nor Greek, there is neither slave nor free person, there is not male and female; for you are all one in Christ Jesus."[167]

Furthermore, the gender equality issue in case study 3 is, as in case study 2, not restricted to the concerns of one individual. The case draws attention to the collective dimension of a pre-existing discriminatory element which affects not only women, but also, and to an equal degree, male faithful who would welcome all clerics with a priestly vocation, regardless of gender. This is also a response to the growing shortage of priests and the recent wave of public scandals in the Catholic Church.

Finally, the balance of competing interests raises the question of whether the implementation of gender equality (in case study 3 the elimination of the pre-existing discriminatory element) would be a greater disadvantage for the election of the parish priest than the traditional standpoint of the church. One disadvantage is the unresolved problem under canon law that the duties of the parish administrator require an ordained minister. The case of the parish of Röschenz[168] concerned a similar problem: In the period when his canonical mission was revoked, the priestly duties of F.S., who continued to act as parish administrator, were unclear under canon law. Against this disadvantage, general equality would have deliv-

---

[163] See among the extensive literature *Schüssler Fiorenza*, pp. 152 ff.; *Raming*, Ausschluss, pp. 166 ff.

[164] *Strahm/Rudolf,* p. 45; see also *Wijngaards,* pp. 113 ff.; *Daly,* pp. 33, 118 ff.

[165] See among others *Eisen*, passim; *Taschl-Erber*, pp. 161 ff.; *Felber*, pp. 197 ff.; *Schüngel-Straumann*, Anfänge, passim; *Schüngel-Straumann,* Eva, pp. 74 ff.; *Ranke-Heinemann*, pp. 264 ff.; *Moltmann-Wendel*, passim; *Heinzelmann*, pp. 81 ff.; *Gössmann* et al., pp. 33 ff. (female apostles), pp. 91 ff. (deaconesses), pp. 455 ff. (female priesthood); *Pemsel-Maier* et al., pp. 21 ff., 40 ff., 58 ff.; *Reininger*, pp. 56 ff.; *Schüssler Fiorenza*, pp. 154 ff.; *Stofer*, pp. 176 ff.

[166] *Raming*, Gleichrangig, p. 3; *Schüssler Fiorenza*, pp. 167 ff. refers to the passage as a "key theological text".

[167] Gal 3: 27 f.

[168] See chap. 1.5.

ered two benefits. On the one hand a pre-existing discriminatory element would not have played a role in the election and, on the other, the elected female candidate, whose performance in office the local church authorities approved of, could have continued to lead the parish, which had clearly expressed its solidarity with her.

However, this still does not remedy the problem under canon law. Therefore, the overall context of the problem needs to be examined.

In a *responsum to the question of ordination* in 1995 the Congregation for the Doctrine of the Faith declared that the Pope's teaching on the non-admission of women belongs to the deposit of faith. This gave the decision the status of infallibility.[169] Hence, at the legal level it could be maintained that the issue of the non-admission of women to the priesthood affects the very substance of religious freedom, which may not be touched. However, internal church priorities can be translated into legal categories only if the corresponding church statement complies with lawful standards. Non-admission of women to the priesthood must be in pursuit of a lawful objective.[170] A lawful objective of this nature, however, cannot be recognised. Although it is a fact that, owing to its patriarchal history, male priesthood – and parallel gender dominance in the secular social sphere – was able to survive for centuries, a lawful objective cannot be constructed on the basis of this long tradition. Religious doctrines cannot enjoy protection as fundamental rights if they pursue objectives that are in flagrant opposition to other fundamental rights. The state has primacy in issues of lawfulness. In this respect, in weighing up competing interests between two conflicting fundamental rights in which one fundamental right is exercised in the absence of a lawful objective this fact must be taken into account to the disadvantage of the party exercising the right.

Despite national and international standards of gender equality, the state will not (at the present time) take the initiative in the issue of the lack of a Roman Catholic female priesthood and apply the appropriate regulations to the Roman Catholic Church. What would, however, be conceivable are constellations similar to those in the case studies, in which a public court has to weigh up the competing interests between the principle of gender equality and religious communities' right to self-determination in individual cases.

---

169 See *Strahm/Rudolf*, p. 38; see, however, the lack of competence of the Congregation for the Doctrine of the Faith to declare a teaching infallible, *Demel*, pp. 81 ff.

170 *Freivogel,* Art. 3 note 28. See also the wording of Art. 140 in conjunction with 137 III sentence 1 (Weimar Constitution) of the Basic Law of the Federal Republic of Germany: "Religious societies shall regulate and administer their affairs independently within the limits of the law that applies to all." See also fn. 27 above. The so-called Church Clause in the German Equal Treatment Act (§ 9 para. 1 Equal Treatment Act – AGG) refers to the fact that religious communities can customise employment contracts according to the religion of the applicant if this is warranted by the type of activity. This special regulation applies only to the criterion religion and not to the criterion gender.

Decisions in favour of the principle of gender equality have to respect proportionality. As a single court decision does not impose a general obligation to introduce the female priesthood, the purely legal effect of such rulings is limited. This must be distinguished from the potentially more far-reaching consequences of a decision by a public court in favour of gender equality, for instance voluntary paradigm shifts in the Church.

In the aforementioned case of Catholic community of Röschenz, the bishop and the parish priest were officially reconciled after the court ruling.[171] Following the decision of the cantonal court, which declared the revocation of the canonical mission to be without effect, the diocese could have re-opened the procedure of privation and re-instated the "rebellious" parish priest in all rights of co-determination demanded by the court. The church authorities could have concluded that on account of the public criticism, which the parish priest did not dispute, a relationship of trust, and hence the basis for a canonical mission, no longer existed. On such evidence in a second attempt they could have presented more comprehensive grounds for revocation. The probability that the court would once again have rejected the detailed reasoning for revocation would have been very small. However, by seeking public reconciliation with the parish priest and re-instating him in his ministry without any reservation, the Church authorities chose a form of maximum option.

The issue of admitting women to leading religious ministries is ultimately a question of status rather than of empowering them to enter totally new fields of activity. Today female theologians already enjoy far-reaching competencies as parish administrators. Through their access to the sanctuary and their priest-like presence at religious services, women have already established a decisive presence that has been accepted by the community. Ultimately, therefore, the step to complete equality for women in the issue of admission to the priesthood is objectively not very large, even though "subjectively" it seems much further-reaching. It is essential, however, that a result which gives priority to the right of gender equality over an objective whose lawfulness cannot be proved should also fulfil the requirement of proportionality.

4.3.3. Summary of the arguments and conclusion

In summary, on the issue of whether a pre-existing discriminatory element can result in the annulment of the election of a female parish administrator, the following arguments support the argument against the church's right to self-determination:

- Gender equality can on principle not be qualified because it would otherwise be inequality; in weighing up competing interests this circumstance would have to

[171] On 29 September 2008 the then Bishop of Basel reinstated F.S.'s canonical mission and confirmed him as parish administrator.

be compensated for by exceptionally weighty grounds in favour of the church's right to self-determination. In the case of the election of a female parish leader (ordained *contra legem*) who has served several terms of office, such exceptionally weighty grounds do not exist, especially as the scope of a positive ruling in favour of gender equality is restricted in respect of both time and place.

- The similar appearance of a female parish leader and an ordained priest in the church is not sufficient ground to conclude that gender equality has been achieved. On the other hand, the acceptance of the woman in the sanctuary may be taken as consensus among the faithful about the admission of women to all offices.
- A positive ruling on gender equality in case study 3 does not mean that the Roman Catholic Church has to introduce the female priesthood. The state intervention is restricted to precluding a pre-existing discriminatory element in the re-election of a female parish leader who was ordained *contra legem*.
- Today, the question of whether the right to gender equality should play a role in appointments to leading religious offices should be asked from the reverse perspective. Theology, too, now questions the exclusion of women from important religious offices and the concomitant inconsistency in respect of the principle of gender equality. The reasons for exclusion are no longer part of God's plan, but are to be found in the historical, patriarchal background of the long, undisputed tradition of reserving priestly ordination to men, the advance of maleness in the expansion of the Church as a strictly hierarchical organisation in the centuries immediately following Christ's death and the exaggerated emphasis on the male gender. In addition, evidence of women holding office was systematically erased (e.g. the existence of female apostles, deaconesses and women in priestly functions in the early church).
- At issue in case study 3, as in case study 2, is not a single individual's concern about gender equality, but collective unequal treatment which, moreover, fails to take account of the emerging shortage of priests and the uneasiness of many of the faithful about a church that is latently organised as a male association.
- Canonical unlawfulness in a case of gender equality cannot play a decisive role in weighing up competing interests as the exclusion of women from the priesthood is not a lawful objective.

Given these arguments, a court could come to the conclusion that gender, and thus exclusion from ordination, may not be ignored in the question of the validity of the election.

Chapter 5 Consequences and outlook

Throughout their history, religious communities regularly redefine themselves without abandoning their core beliefs. This is intimately connected with the fact that any religious genesis calls for interpretation from the moment it comes into existence. While outward expression may change, the core remains. In other words, it is from the outset a complex cosmos – manifested in Christianity in the shape of a human being (Jesus), in Islam and Judaism in the form of a message from God (Qu'ran and Torah) – the comprehension of which need not be immediate, complete and eternal. Thus, it can adapt over time and is open to interpretation and reinterpretation. At the same time, this hermeneutic dimension raises the issue of power: who sanctions interpretation? The answer is obvious: the religious leaders have the final say. For centuries this authority went undisputed, a structural side-effect of historical patriarchal circumstances. With the rise of the gender-equality debate in the twentieth and twentieth-first centuries, this ultimately self-asserted male claim to authority was also up for discussion – not so much because the leaders were deprived of their authority, but because opposing opinions coalesced and ultimately prevailed. The original consensus has gradually given way to dissent, a development that plays a role in weighting an argument.

In the meantime, gender equality has become a fundamental right that calls for universal applicability. This is particularly striking in the European debate about Islam, in which the renunciation of discriminatory practices is a relatively uncompromising postulate both inside and outside the European Community.

It is not the role of the law to dictate content, but to develop *methods* to achieve a balance between conflicting interests manifest in very diverse communities that is as considerate of all interests as possible. Owing to tradition this will also include taboo zones, one of which is the relationship between law and religion with respect to women in general and to their exclusion from the priesthood in the Roman Catholic Church in particular.

Consideration of women's rights in religious communities within a legal context raises a number of questions. The first is whether the law is applicable to a sphere of life in which transcendental content plays a defining role. The next is whether a discriminatory constellation is present. If both questions are answered in the affirmative (as I have tried to do in chapters 1 and 2), the next problem is to explore whether discrimination in respect of admission to leading spiritual offices can be viewed as a conflict between the right to gender equality and the right to religious freedom. Once these preliminaries have been settled, attention turns to the central task of drawing up a list of the arguments and juxtaposing and weighing up the conflicting standpoints. The conclusion to be drawn from the analysis of the arguments and counterarguments conducted in chapters 3 and 4 is that today the principle of gender equality should be given greater weight than the appeal to a long-standing tradition of male officeholders, a phenomenon common to all three world religions. I have listed the various arguments and their weighting according to objective criteria, i.e., in effect performed an analysis *lege artis*. Hence, they can be checked and verified. The three case studies have not occurred as described. But the possibility that a court of law will at some point have to rule on a case with a similar constellation involving gender equality law cannot be excluded.

The canonical procedure for the excommunication of the seven women who were ordained as Roman Catholic priests was based on the legal sanctions available under canon law (CIC).[172] The Congregation for the Doctrine of the Faith issued a written warning of excommunication,[173] against which the women made recourse, as is provided for in the CIC.[174] The women also made recourse against the decree of excommunication issued by the Congregation shortly afterwards on 5 August 2002. Instead of forwarding this appeal to the next highest judicial authority, the Supreme Tribunal of the Apostolic Signatura, the Congregation rejected the appeal in a decree of 21 December 2002, in which it simultaneously confirmed the excommunication.[175] The procedure was flawed on procedural grounds[176] that have never been addressed. The most serious ground is that the procedure as conducted failed to grant the accused an opportunity to defend themselves. The excommunication was *ferendae sententiae*, a so-called imposed penalty,[177] which requires that in judicial proceedings the accused be given an opportunity for defence.[178] *Demel* records that

---

172 For a detailed account see *Demel*, pp. 93 ff. In 2007 attempted female ordination was declared a punishable offence; see *Demel* (2012), pp. 201 ff.

173 Ordered in a letter of the Congregation for the Doctrine of the Faith, called a monitum (warning), published in *Demel*, p. 94.

174 *Demel*, p. 99.

175 The two decrees are published in *Demel*, pp. 100, 105 ff.

176 For a detailed account see Demel, pp. 97 f. (monitum of 10 July 2002), p. 101 (decree of 5 August 2002), pp. 108 ff. (decree of 21 December 2002).

177 The *ferendae sententiae* penalty must be imposed through a church tribunal (see *Demel*, p. 95).

178 Can. 1720 (1); see *Demel*, p. 110.

in this case they were not, which is "clearly a legal infringement"[179]. Next, the final decree of 21 December 2002 was issued by a non-competent authority, especially as the appeal by the accused should have been forwarded to the Supreme Tribunal of the Apostolic Signatura.[180] Finally, to prevent the use of any other legal remedy against its decree of 21 December 2002 the Congregation approved passage of a papal decree *in forma specifica*, although canon law does not provide for special approval by the Pope in this form in decisions of the Congregation for the Doctrine of the Faith in individual cases.[181] However, pursuant to this approval another provision of the CIC took effect, viz that there is neither appeal nor recourse against a judgment or a decree of the Roman Pontiff.[182] Hence, because of the papal approval *in forma specifica* all legal remedies against the judgment of excommunication issued by a non-competent authority were excluded, even though the accused women were unable to exercise their right to defend themselves, as is usual in criminal procedural law and also provided for in the CIC.[183]

Penal proceedings in which people accused of a "most serious offence"[184] are not granted an opportunity for defence infringes the most basic claim to fairness. This also applies to proceedings under canon law, particularly as the CIC also provides for this possibility for defence. It is difficult to understand why the flaws in the excommunication procedure have not been more widely criticised. One reason suggested in the literature was that because "the facts are unequivocal"[185] the case lacked the "suspense"[186] of a contest between the prosecution and the defence that often marks proceedings of this nature. Such statements fail, however, to recognise the fundamental importance of a fair trial. It is irrelevant whether people not involved in the proceedings describe facts in advance as unequivocal. The sense and purpose of legal proceedings is to examine each and every unequivocal fact by examining the position, the standpoint and the evidence of the accused. The accused may not be degraded[187] to an object of the proceedings; rather he must be able to participate in them. That is the logical consequence of a concept of man that is based on the dignity of the individual and guarantees him or her a fair trial.

---

179 *Demel*, p. 110.

180 *Demel*, p. 111.

181 Special approval by the Pope is possible only if a decision of the Congregation for the Doctrine of the Faith contains a general enactment; see *Demel*, p. 108.

182 Can. 333 § 3; *Demel*, p. 109.

183 These were not the only procedural irregularities; on the other flaws see *Demel* pp. 97 ff., 101, 108 ff.

184 Decree of Excommunication of the Congregation for the Doctrine of the Faith of 5 August 2002.

185 *Demel*, p. 106.

186 *Demel*, p. 105.

187 *Hafner/Brosi*, p. 151.

The somewhat defeatist acceptance of the excommunication proceedings against the female priests *contra legem* also highlights another aspect. It is astonishing that the use of can. 1024 CIC as the crucial argument has gone virtually unchallenged – notwithstanding the discourse on universal human rights – and conclusions drawn about the *unequivocal nature of the situation*.[188] One can think of a more creative approach to this legal rule. Why not start a discussion among the faithful on how to embed the regulation in the contemporary human rights context by reformulating the provision so as to avoid any mention of gender? The regulation can. 1024 CIC would continue to require baptism as a prerequisite for the priesthood; at the same time the gender issue would remain open, which could create scope for new possibilities. This in turn could bring new life into the exegesis by taking up the approach of the Pontifical Biblical Commission, according to which the text of the Bible itself contains no grounds for the non-admission of women to the priesthood. From here to looking for biblical evidence of the priestly ordination of baptised women would be a small step for exegesis, but a huge step for a religious community in the twenty-first century.

I am still hopeful that the religious communities will achieve gender equality in their ranks through their own efforts and, in consequence, the Roman Catholic Church will introduce the female priesthood. It has already taken the initial step in respect of celibacy: the admission of married men as permanent deacons[189] caused relatively few problems.

---

[188] See e.g. *Demel*, pp. 61 f., 100.
[189] See *Brosi*, p. 149.

Interviews

The following interviews complement the legal section. Three experts from different academic backgrounds express their views about gender equality in the religious sphere. All three women were asked the same legal questions – adapted, where appropriate, to take account of the religious background of each interviewee.

A. The way women are treated is a crime

Ida Raming, born 1932 in Fürstenau, Germany, D.Th., Catholic theologian, teacher and author; petitioner to the Second Vatican Council (1962–1965); one of seven female theologians who were ordained to the Roman Catholic priesthood by Roman Catholic Bishop Rómulo Antonio Braschi in 2002; excommunicated on 21 December 2002; numerous articles and publications on the position of women in the Roman Catholic Church and the non-admission of women to the priesthood.

Interview with Dr Ida Raming

1) Question: Contrary to can. 1024 CIC, according to which only a baptised man validly receives sacred ordination, you were ordained as a Catholic priest. How do you justify the action *contra legem*?

Ida Raming (I. R.): Before Iris Müller, another theologian, and I took this step, we spent more than 40 years studying all aspects of and fighting for the ordination of women. We submitted a petition to the Second Vatican Council calling for equality for women in the diaconate and the priesthood. My doctoral dissertation, many articles and several books have dealt with the topic of the non-admission of women to the priesthood and the historical and present situation of women in the Church.

The Vatican's response to all arguments and efforts was always negative: in 1977 the negation of women in the priesthood in *Inter Insigniores*, in 1994 the definitive no in *Ordinatio Sacerdotalis*. We realised that further argument would be useless and that what we were dealing with in the exclusion of women was not a question of truth, but of entrenched gender-based discrimination and the question of power.

Hence, we decided to take a public stand against existing canon law and acted in accordance with the Biblical principle: "We must obey God rather than men" (Acts 5:29). In our action we also invoked Jesus, who also violated religious laws and Sabbath rules that did not serve the people.

Moreover, there are twentieth century "precedents" for this action: already in 1970 Catholic Bishop Felix Davídek ordained women as deans and priests in the Czech underground Church contrary to existing canon law.[190] At the time there were pastoral grounds for this action. Priests in the underground Church who wanted, for example, to care for people in custody, could on entering a prison easily be unmasked by the Communists and arrested on the spot. There was less danger when women visited prisoners for the simple reason that no one suspected that these women were ordained priests of the underground Church. Davídek also consistently advocated the ordination of women as priests in the Roman Catholic Church, not only when special circumstances merited it.

2) Question: Is there any self-reflection in Roman Catholic theology about the contents of its faith? Is it possible to interpret theologically relevant, sacred texts and internal Church laws in a way that is relevant to modern society?

I. R.: That is actually the business of professors (men and women) in theological faculties. They have to interpret the Biblical texts in a manner that makes

---

[190] See *Peter Sepp*, Geheime Weihen, Die Frauen in der verborgenen tschechoslowakischen Kirche Koinótēs, Ostfildern 2004.

them relevant to the present. Research in feminist theology has also contributed far-reaching inputs. Scholars have produced solid evidence of deaconesses in the New Testament (e.g. Phoebe). The existence of female apostles could also be proved (e.g. Priska and Junia). The latter was long thought to be a man. Junia was turned into a Junias. Scholars were able to show that Junia was a common woman's name, whereas the man's name Junias does not exist.

However, the question is whether the results of this exegesis and dogmatics are accepted "at the top". Will the Congregation for the Doctrine of the Faith adopt the results of biblical gender studies? In the 1970s the Congregation for the Doctrine of the Faith of the Roman Catholic Church commissioned the Pontifical Biblical Commission to research Bible teaching on female ordination.

In 1976 the Pontifical Biblical Commission reached conclusions that were favourable towards women: the New Testament does not offer any viable reason in principle against the admission of women to the ministerial priesthood. The Congregation for the Doctrine of the Faith did not approve of the conclusions of its own commission; therefore, they were ignored and archived.

In other words, self-reflection at the scientific level does indeed take place, but is controlled "from the top" and ultimately often circumvented. Although lay people also have religious convictions and can contribute to self-reflection, to date this has always been left to experts, who then write until their fingers ache without finding a hearing in Rome, let alone acceptance. The official Church body responsible for self-reflection, the Congregation for the Doctrine of the Faith, is obviously interested only in preserving its position of power, which, logically, is the status quo.

3) Question: Looking at discrimination in the Roman Catholic Church against the background of fundamental rights, we encounter the problem of the conflict between the right to self-determination or freedom of religion and the principle of gender equality. Juridical weighting of the arguments in the weighingup of competing interests during proceedings in a public court could conceivably tip the scales in favour of the principle of gender equality. Do you consider a juridical solution to the issue of women's rights in the Roman Catholic Church appropriate? Do you think state law should play a crucial role in the context of religious issues?

I. R.: We should at least try this path. Only time will tell if it is expedient. However, it may raise people's awareness of the discrimination and legal inequalities that women face in the Roman Catholic Church. This, in turn, may bring a degree of pressure to bear on the Church hierarchy. All over the world people are increasingly demanding recognition of their human rights – which include the free choice of occupation – and this also applies to the Roman Catholic Church.

But there is also another approach. In more and more cases plaintiffs are claiming their fundamental rights within the religious sphere. Let us take the case of an organist employed in a Catholic church. He divorces his wife and marries or lives with another woman. Because his private life is no longer in accordance with Catholic moral teachings, the Church seeks to dismiss him. When the man appeals against his dismissal before a labour court, the court has to decide which right should be weighted more heavily: the Church's right to self-determination or a person's fundamental right of free choice of life partner. If the number of rulings of this kind increases, this could set the ball rolling.

4) Question: Up to now, the legal community, too, has not taken the weighing up of competing interests to its logical conclusion. The proceedings have usually ended with the observation that a Church's right to self-determination carries a lot of weight. From your point of view as a theologian, how much weight should be given to the Church's right to self-determination?

I. R.: In the context of the issue of women's rights, not much thought has, in my opinion, been given to the matter. Dietmar Mieth, a professor of moral theology, made an important observation in 1996: he noted that the church as "an institution created by God with our involvement" that works in the public realm may not lag behind institutional justice. And human rights are part of this institutional justice.

In this connection I should like to point out contradictions within canon law itself. According to can. 385 CIC the diocesan bishop bears responsibility for fostering vocations, in particular the "priestly and missionary vocations". According to can. 1026 CIC it is forbidden to deter a person who is "canonically suitable" from receiving orders. When, however, the competent church officials admit only men to the priestly ministry, they are telling God that God's spirit calls only men to the priesthood.

There are other contradictions between the at least rudimentary formulation of fundamental rights in the CIC and the non-admission of women to the priesthood. In this context one may mention, for instance, can. 219 CIC, which formulates the fundamental right to freedom in choosing a state of life. The freedom to choose a state of life allows women to live a life as clerics.

It was not inferred from the circumstance that all of the apostles were Jewish that only Jews could be admitted to the priesthood. Now, it should not be forgotten that its Jewish origins played a very significant role in the early Church. With good reason one could have said that all superior Church officials must be Jewish or prove they are of Jewish descent.

Can. 849 CIC is also relevant in this context: "Baptism, the gateway to the sacraments (. . .)" – which includes the sacrament of holy orders! In other words:

both women and men are baptised; women are also baptised and as such they may not be excluded from the sacraments.

Nor should the important message in Gal. 3:28 be overlooked, which emphasises the fundamental equality of all baptised persons in Christ, irrespective of their gender. In interpreting this passage from the Bible, however, the Church used a trick. "Yes", say the church authorities, "we know all that: in heaven women are equal to men, but not on earth." As you can see, the Church leaders always find a way out!

In my personal opinion, human rights should set limits to religious communities' right to self-determination. I believe that disregard of human rights runs counter both to God's purpose and to a proper understanding of Christianity. Baptism is the decisive criterion, not gender, a fact that is also expressed in canon law (can. 849 CIC).

5) Question: The weighing up in law of competing interests involves weighing up the different interests on both sides. The procedure continues until it is possible to deliver a reasoned statement in favour of either self-determination of the religious community or recognition of the principle of equality. In your opinion, which criteria need to be taken into account in this matter?

I. R.: In my view, the observance of human rights has the greater weight in this debate: prohibition of gender discrimination, the right to free choice of occupation and the right to training.

We Catholic female theologians do not even have a right to comprehensive training. There are women who would like to train as priests and attend specific courses in a seminary. But they are refused admission. Here, too, it may be possible to build a legal case that would have to be decided by a court of law.

An interesting situation in a German diocese illustrates this point. A teacher of religion was ordained a deaconess *contra legem*. Thereupon her permission to teach religion was revoked. At the same time she continued to perform various Church ministries in the parish such as first ministrant and preacher, partly because, given the shortage of priests, nobody else was available.

The issue became public when a local broadcaster asked to make a film with her. On learning of this, the diocesan bishop forbade her to perform any further church ministries, let alone be filmed doing so. The judicial vicar, i.e. the canon lawyer of the ordinariate, formally discussed the issue with her. He then wrote a letter to the Vatican, noting that this religion teacher had already performed a great number of services for the Church; at the same time, she admitted that she had agreed to diaconal ordination *contra legem*. Rome should decide what should be done about this woman!

The bishop summoned her once again and said: "Just say: 'I am sorry, I should not have agreed to diaconal ordination.' I shall then set a period, and if in this time you say nothing about the admission of women to the priesthood you will be allowed to teach religion again." The religion teacher did not want to accept this. The Vatican has yet to respond.

I adopted another approach with my petition to the Federal German parliament. I addressed the topic of state appropriations in favour of the Roman Catholic Church, in particular the financing of episcopal sees. We women are excluded from the episcopate, yet bishops receive public grants. Is the state willing to protect our claim to equal rights?

In the meantime, I have received a negative reply from the Committee on Petitions. The state is "not causally" and also "not indirectly" responsible for the violation of Art. 3 of the Federal German constitution.[191]

Not only leading clergymen, but all members of the Church should be heard on the question of self-determination. At present the argument of the religious community's right to self-determination is used only by the Church hierarchy – regardless of the opinions of other members of the Church, in particular women. As baptised people they are also the Church and as such they must also be heard and be able to decide.

6) Question: One possibility, for example, would be to weigh up the competing interests from the point of view of utility, in other words, to ask where the *greater* utility lies: in enforcing the principle of gender equality or for the Roman Catholic Church to continue its practice of reserving priesthood to men? Is there greater utility in maintaining an almost two-thousand-year-old tradition of the priesthood for men? Or is there greater utility in admitting people who, regardless of gender, feel they have a vocation for the priestly ministry? Do you think this question brings us any further?

I. R.: In my opinion it is obvious that enforcing the principle of gender equality is more beneficial for the Church. In his 1963 encyclical *Pacem in terris* Pope John XXIII called on people to recognise the "signs of the times"; in his opinion this expressly included the fact that women should claim the rights and duties that are in keeping with their dignity as human beings.

In contrast, the permanent exclusion of women will lead to ossification in the Church. Its impact on the development of men as well as women as people is very negative: male hubris and gender arrogance on the one hand and stunted growth

[191] Art 3 (2) of the Basic Law of the Federal Republic of Germany states: " Men and women are equal. The state supports the effective realization of equality of women and men and works towards abolishing present disadvantages."

of the female personality on the other – all of which harms the human community and the Church.

I personally look back on many years of experience as an excluded woman. On account of non-admission to the priesthood women in the Roman Catholic Church are in many ways stunted and severely restricted in the development of their competencies and skills, and that also affects the individual. Women often lack the profile of people with a well-rounded training and education. They are often still appendages of men, have adapted themselves and do not stand up for what they really think. The traditional female idea that a woman can "shine" or impress particularly through her sexuality and her female body remains so powerful because there are few uplifting spiritual or religious role models for women. To this extent, the way women are treated is a crime. And then the Catholic Church authorities still insist: We have always emphasised the dignity of women! They may be virgins, nuns and mothers. They still propagate this blinkered approach today. In other words, the fact that today women work in many different occupations and every job should in principle be open to them – including the priesthood – is not part of the vision or the intention of the Church hierarchy.

When we decided to take ordination *contra legem* we were seven women in all. Today there are already about 150 of us (as of October 2012). And with God's help and the working of God's Holy Spirit, which we hope may guide our actions, our numbers will continue to grow!

The interview with Dr Ida Raming took place in Asemwald/Stuttgart, where the theologian lives in busy retirement, on 18 December 2012.

Glossary

1977 Inter Insigniores	Declaration of the Congregation for the Doctrine of the Faith on the impossibility of admitting women to the ministerial priesthood (confirmed by the then Pope)
1994 Ordinatio Sacerdotalis	Apostolic Letter of Pope John Paul II "on reserving priestly ordination to men alone" and the definitiveness of this judgment
Acts	Acts of the Apostles, fifth book of the New Testament
Congregation for the Doctrine of the Faith	Central authority of the Roman Catholic Church to defend the Church from deviations in official Church teaching; formerly called the Inquisition
Pontifical Biblical Commission	Group of experts within the Congregation for the Doctrine of the Faith, consisting of official biblical scholars; in an evaluation it negated the existence of biblical grounds for excluding women from the priesthood
CIC	Codex Iuris Canonici, Code of Canon Law, codification of canonical legislation for the Roman Catholic Church (canon law); last completely revised in 1983
can.	Canon, provision in the CIC
Gal.	Epistle of Paul to the Galations, New Testament (Gal. 3:28: "There is neither Jew nor Greek, there is neither slave nor free person, there is not male and female: for you are all one in Christ Jesus.")

B. Dina d'malkhuta dina – an old rabbinical principle could facilitate the breakthrough for gender equality

Bea Wyler, born in 1951 in Baden (Switzerland), studied agricultural engineering at ETH Zurich, various activities in the media sector, trained for the rabbinate in London and New York, ordained in 1995; rabbi of the congregations in Oldenburg and Brunswick and university lecturer in Jewish studies; working as an independent rabbi in Switzerland since 2004.

Interview with Rabbi Bea Wyler

1) Question: You were lawfully ordained in 1995, yet are still the only woman active as a rabbi in Switzerland. Can one speak of discrimination in leading Jewish spiritual offices?

Bea Wyler (B. W.): In Orthodox congregations I could not expect to be appointed rabbi – for the simple reason that I am a woman. These congregations would also justify their position in the same way: women cannot be rabbis. To which I reply: the rabbis who ordained me knew what they were doing. The response to this is – at best – a shrug of the shoulders. This is a way of not explicitly saying: "We do not want a woman as rabbi."

2) Question: Are there differences in status between women and men in the practice of worship?

B. W.: Women do indeed have a second-class status in the Orthodox worship service: they do not count in the Minyan (the quorum for a religious service). Women are also not called upon to read from the Torah and may not serve as prayer leader at a religious service. At religious services, including family-centred celebrations such as a Bar Mitzvah, women and men sit apart. Nor may women say Kaddish on the death of a family member,[192] as the congregation would not respond – despite the fact that such a shared prayer often has a powerful therapeutic effect in a time of grief. Women are still denied this and many other functions.

Referring to Minyan, you should know that Minyan means community, means public. Praying in the community carries greater spiritual weight than praying on one's own. Hence, it is desirable to perform prayer in the congregation. Now, if a woman cannot be counted as Minyan because of her gender, she always has to pray alone, never with the congregation. If at the same time the congregation says that praying in the congregation is better than praying in private, this is a massive discrimination. Of course, there is a historical explanation of why women do not count in the Minyan. The reason is practical. The morning service of worship can take place as early as six o'clock, which makes it practically impossible for a mother with small children to participate.

The Torah itself does not prohibit women from praying; indeed, the Torah contains few provisions governing regular prayer practice. By contrast, there are certain exegetic texts from which such discriminatory rules can (but need not) be derived.

---

[192] See *Wyler*, pp. 229 ff.

3) Question: You take the view that the issue of gender equality in the twenty-first century, in other words including the female rabbinate, is compatible with three thousand years of Jewish tradition. How do you explain that?

B.W.: This is the point to ask the question, as has been asked, whether the laws of the Halakha, which were formulated in a specific historical context, can be read in a modern sense. This is how I see it. We are not betraying traditions if we ask questions in a different way. And there are thoroughly modern and contemporary answers.

A good example is the morning prayer, a daily ritual, not just at Shabbat. We Jews have a duty to pray three times a day, almost like a medication! It would be more satisfactory if everyone could pray with the congregation. But many families have small children to take care of. Now if you say that the woman does not go to communal prayer because she has duties of care at home, whereas it is taken for granted that the man attends communal prayer, then we have a problem. If the solution to this problem is to release women who have time-related duties of care from the duty of prayer, a problem of logistics and time becomes one of gender discrimination. It is simple to remedy this without sacrificing tradition, or even giving up privileges. For example: Releasing the member of the couple who takes care of the children from the duty to attend morning prayer, while allowing the other member of the couple to fulfil it (for the entire family), will eliminate the discrimination. In this way child care and observance of the duty of prayer are treated as equivalent aspects of religious life that are not tied to gender. I have experienced this practice in New York congregations.

4) Question: So you could say that there are no legal provisions, like canon law in the Roman Catholic Church, that prevent gender equality. Rather in Orthodox congregations it is primarily the influence of historical, patriarchal practices. How is your ordination viewed in the context of Jewish law?

B. W.: I was ordained at the Jewish Theological Seminary (JTS) of the Conservative Movement of America, which had just celebrated its centenary at the time of my ordination. A special commission consisting of the faculty of the JTS and the rabbinate was appointed to study the legal issue of whether women could be ordained rabbis, and after careful consideration it concluded that they could. Some faculty members left the Seminary on account of this decision. The ordination of women as rabbis did not take place overnight, and even today is still impossible in some religious movements within Judaism.

There are a number of indications at different places in rabbinical literature of what is required of a scholar to fulfil the office of rabbi. But nowhere is it written that it is reserved to men. Naturally, this reflects the fact that the question of whether women can be rabbis is a twentieth-century question. And in the twentieth century, after careful study of the scriptures the question was answered in the affirmative. To be an active rabbi means first and foremost study; the rabbi is in the first place a scholar and a teacher. The other activities follow: leading religious services, spiritual care, presence at the major events in people's lives (birth, Bar Mitzvah, marriage and burial) and other duties in the local rabbinate.

In Judaism, each religious movement has dealt with the issue of women for itself, in other words the Conservative Movement for itself, Orthodox Judaism for itself, the congregations in America for themselves, those in Europe for themselves and those in Israel for themselves. There is no "Vatican" in Judaism, whereby the (Orthodox) Chief Rabbinate of Israel perceives itself as a kind of universal authority. But outside of Israel it is not recognised as the final instance. Since the congregations are autonomous, the final say always lies with the local rabbi.

5) Question: Is there a place in Jewish theology for discussion and self-reflection on the contents of faith? If so, who discusses and reflects on it: theological experts? The clergy? Congregants? Is it possible to interpret the theologically relevant texts (Holy Scripture and the code of religious rules) in modern terms?

B. W.: Judaism *is* interpretation. If we assume that the Torah is of divine origin, yet we are able to understand it only with our human understanding and explain it only with our human speech, then every explanation is an interpretation. As each person who interprets has a different personal background, each interpretation is always a little different. Interpretation means: the text is given, but the interpretation is open. My examination sermon, for instance, was about the history of the rape of the daughter of Jacob and Leah, which ends in a horrible bloodbath. I used this passage from the first book of Moses, Genesis, to talk about domestic violence and how we should deal with it in our Jewish communities. Such approaches are rare in the Talmud.

What I want to say is that it takes the experience of all sections of the population to interpret the Torah; only in this way can the interpretation illuminate all facets. Through their experiences women have made substantial contributions to the interpretation of the Torah. When we as a Jewish community hear all these experiences and think about them, this is extremely enriching for the Jewish tradition of interpretation and, put simply, doubles it. For this reason alone, further progress toward gender equality in the rabbinate is desirable.

In the Siddur, the Orthodox Jewish prayer book, there is, for example, this sentence:

"Thanks be to God, I was not born a woman."

At this point the women say:

"Thanks be to God for creating me according to His will."

In the meantime, there are also Orthodox prayer books that omit the offensive sentence that the men pray. In my opinion, the men's sentence should be deleted without substitution and the women's sentence should serve as the sentence for everyone. What harm is there for a man to thank God for creating him according to God's will?! Modern interpretation is possible in all areas of life, but it is essential particularly in respect of contemporary issues if we want Judaism to be lived within the modern world. These issues include, for example, environmental protection, organic food, political correctness, and gender equality – how can these topics be reflected in the Jewish world?

6) Question: Considering gender discrimination within a religious community from a human-rights perspective leads to the problem of a clash or discrepancy between the self-determination of the religious community and international legal standards of gender equality. This discrepancy has a constitutional dimension, and a balance needs to be struck between self-determination and the implementation of gender equality. By seeking such a balance, one might come to the conclusion that the good of achieving gender equality outweighs any (essentially patriarchal) religious traditions. But do you think that state law should play a crucial role in the context of religious issues? Do you consider a legal solution to the issue of women's rights in religious communities appropriate?

B. W.: The law can be very meaningful in religious communities. Today, one can make a good case for a ban on *shechita* if the animal is not stunned beforehand. In the case of filling offices I see things a little differently. Despite the validity of the principle of gender equality, a congregation should have the right to determine whom they want to employ as rabbi. And if, for reasons of political correctness, someone is dissatisfied that his congregation either can or will not have a woman in the rabbinate, he should probably look for a congregation in which this issue has been decided in favour of women. Backing down is one thing, living according to one's convictions another.

I am confident that little strokes fell big oaks. Once when I was talking to an Orthodox rabbi, he told me that in the Orthodox rabbinate, too, he sees duties that women could fulfil. To which I responded that I agreed with him entirely: all – all duties in the rabbinate can be fulfilled by women. But I did not say that every woman and every man is equally well-suited for all duties.

Perhaps it is best to start in a large congregation that has more than one rabbi. Such a congregation could set a good example and say: we deploy our rabbis, whether men or women, on the basis of ability. I, for one, am a moderate pastoral counsellor, but a very good teacher.

Recruitment is a particular problem. Orthodox congregations do not employ women rabbis because "actually" they cannot exist. A gender-neutrally formulated job advertisement placed by an Orthodox congregation would be a joke: everybody knows that this congregation is looking for a rabbi approved by the Chief Rabbinate of Israel.

Even in the Conservative Movement, which has ordained women as rabbis since 1985, women complain that that congregations looking for a rabbi invite them for a job interview, but at the same time make it plain from the outset that they have no chance of being appointed. The invitation to the job interview is only a concession to political correctness.

Although it can also take a man many years to move from a small congregation to a larger or possibly very large congregation, we have reached that point in time where women rabbis, too, should be filling positions in large congregations. But the figures (even in the USA) tell another story:[193] in Switzerland I am still the first and only women active as a rabbi. In Germany I was not the first, but for many years the only woman rabbi.

If a congregation does not want to move towards gender equality under any circumstances and certain men use power plays to secure their privileges, perhaps modern Jews must turn their back on them and join a more liberal congregation. Today one has such options. Furthermore, changes in infrastructure can also start processes rolling. When declining membership means that institutions like schools and kindergartens are functioning at less than full capacity, orthodox and liberal congregations talk to each other. And vice versa: whereas 30 years ago an orthodox congregation would pressure liberal members to leave, the situation is now the opposite: orthodox congregations would like to work with successful, more liberal congregations. A trial of strength is taking place between the Jewish congregations of the different religious movements, which is not necessarily the worst thing that could happen to the Jewish community.

7) Question: Up to now no state court has weighed the benefits of the self-determination of religious communities against gender equality (for lack of a relevant case). In legal literature you find only the statement that the self-determination of religious communities is of great importance. What priority has self-determination in Judaism, and who defines that priority?

---

[193] Around the year 2000 there were about 600–800 women rabbis; today there are considerably more. In the meantime the Reform and Conservative Movements are ordaining women rabbis in Israel, South America, London and Germany. The Reconstructionist Movement is limited to the USA. Orthodox Judaism still does not ordain women rabbis. Orthodox women ordained as rabbis have been ordained "privately", i.e., ordained by a single rabbi, not by a seminary. This is an option, but is seldom made use of (information from Bea Wyler).

B. W.: Naturally the congregations each claim to have a right to self-determination. That would be in order if all members of a congregation had a say. However, even today there are communities in Switzerland in which women de facto have no voting rights. These communities practise household voting; in other words, voting is not tied to the individual. Only if a woman lives alone in her household is she able to vote independently. This is not an instance of classic gender discrimination, but worse: in the final analysis it is discrimination against married persons, which is, of course, unacceptable in a community in which family life is held in such high regard. Viewed objectively, it is a discrimination of women. I have heard the argument that it is impossible for there to be different views within a family.

8) Question: The legal mechanism of weighing up conflicting interests (self-determination versus achieving gender equality) aims to come to a reasoned conclusion as to whether one position or the other is the decisive factor, so that when a conflict arises, priority should be given to the position with the most convincing arguments. What criteria (arguments), then, should be taken into consideration in this legal "weighing up" of competing interests?

B. W.: A principle in the rabbinical tradition, dina d'malkhuta dina, holds that the law of the land in which one lives is the law. Hence, in any nation the legally codified principle of equality between women and men that should, in accordance with dina d'malchuta dina, be asserted or more widely applied in Jewish congregations as well. As dina d'malkhuta dina is a rabbinical principle, by enforcing gender equality we would act in accordance with classical Jewish tradition. On account of this priority rule, therefore, in the weighing up the conflict of interests gender equality would be accorded great weight. The priority rule or principle should directly impact the issue of how we can shape our life in the community so as to give woman an equal voice, be it in prayer in the congregation or in other activities in the community.

The interview with Rabbi Bea Wyler took place in Basel, where she is helping to found a new liberal congregation, on 15 April 2013.

Glossary

Religious movements in Judaism:	Woman in the rabbinate:
Orthodox Judaism:	Is not (yet) accepted
Reform Judaism:	Is accepted and practised (in both sub-groups, the Reform and the more progressive Liberal movements)
Conservative Movement:	Between Reform and Orthodox Judaism, views Halakha (religious law) as binding; women count in the Minyan (quorum required for public prayer); derived from this is the possibility that women may assume leading functions, e.g. the rabbinate
Minyan	Quorum of at least ten Jewish adults required for certain religious rituals, in particular public prayer; in orthodox congregations women do not count in the Minyan
Torah	In the narrower sense, the books of Moses, the first five books of the Old Testament; in the wider sense, the whole body of traditional Jewish teaching up to the present
Talmud	The Mishnah and the Gemara together form the Talmud; two Talmuds: the older compiled in Israel ("Jerushalmi": Jerusalem or Palestinian Talmud, final recension about 375 CE) and the somewhat younger and more important compiled in Babylon ("Babli": Babylonian Talmud, final recension around 550 CE)
Dina d'malkhuta dina	Rabbinical rule in the Talmud, according to which the law of the land in which one lives is the law
Rabbi	Teacher, who through her/his studies of the Jewish tradition has a greater knowledge than the members of the congregation and uses this knowledge to serve God
Halakha	Collective body of Jewish religious laws compiled in various centres after completion of the Talmuds; the halakhic process is on-going
Bar/Bat Mitzvah	"Son/Daughter of the commandment", attainment of religious majority

C. As a woman one must have the courage to break taboos

Rajaa Naji al Makkawi, born in 1958 in Wazzan (Morocco), PhD, legal expert; Professor of law at Mohammed V University in Rabat-Agdal and president of the Research Unit on Health Law; in 2003 became the first woman to deliver a religious lecture before King Mohammed VI in the Ramadan lecture series; member of numerous commissions on justice reform, including the Committee of Fatwa of the Supreme Council of Ulama of Morocco, Commission on Justice Reform, National Commission for Human Rights; advisor on Morocco's programme to train women as imams (murshidat).

Interview with Rajaa Naji al Makkawi, PhD

1) Question: You are the first woman in the Islamic world to deliver a religious lecture before the king at the most important Ramadan celebrations. Why were you as a legal scholar selected for this honour in these male-dominated religious circles?

Rajaa Naji al Makkawi (R. N. M.): In my legal research – I do research in the fields of health law, family law and criminal law – I always also explore the position taken by Islamic law, for instance on assisted suicide or on organ transplants. The juxtaposition of public (secular) law and Islamic law has become part of my working method.

My interest in Islamic law and these legal comparisons was behind this request to give one of the lectures at the Ramadan lectures, the first woman to do so. Thus, in 2003 an absolute taboo was broken. Never before in the Islamic world had a woman appeared publicly at a Ramadan celebration and held a speech on a religious topic. Up until then, in other words for centuries, such Ramadan lectures were reserved exclusively to men. Moreover, since 2003 the presence of women has been institutionalised: now every year one of the lectures is given by a woman.

2) Question: In Islam do Muslim women face discrimination in admission to the highest spiritual offices? May female Islamic scholars issue a fatwa (legal opinion)?

R. N. M.: There are three levels of Islamic scholars, and women are represented at all three levels. The highest level are the *ulama* and the *alimat* (female legal scholars), who are often university professors. The second level of Islamic scholars is also trained in Islamic law, and at the third level of Islamic scholarship are the imams and their female counterparts, the murshidat.

Although there were female Islamic scholars prior to 2003, in this year the training of murshidat – and imams – in Morocco was institutionalised. The solemn breaking of the taboo in 2003 was also the beginning of a stronger presence of female teachers of religion at all three levels in public. From then on women with a training in Islam had the authority to deliver lectures, give classes and lead discussion groups on topics related to religion in public, i.e., in mosques, schools and prisons. This in turn enabled the religiously interested female population to participate in these new forms of communication. As a result, women have access to serious Qu'ran studies in the public space.

Concerning the fatwa, you should know that the issuing of fatwas was restructured when the present king ascended the throne (1999). A Fatwa Committee was appointed within the Supreme Council of Ulama to prepare the proposals for legal opinions or learned interpretations. Accordingly, such opinions do not reflect the personal viewpoint of a religious scholar. The Supreme Council of Ulama is a body with around 100 members, of which I am one. As a member of the council I receive the various files on my desk and must draft proposals for the religious questions they raise and present them to the full committee. The issue is debated in plenary and at the end the official opinion (fatwa) is issued. Such fatwas are binding on the regional religious councils and Moroccan society, and accordingly have to be convincingly substantiated.

As a woman – even if to date only three women are members of this Supreme Council of Ulama – it is thus possible to make a contribution in the official body that issues fatwas. Female specialists in religion can also deal with Islamic topics in scientific publications and formulate their view of things. In such cases these are personal standpoints and not fatwas.

3) Question: Can a woman as imam lead Friday prayer in the mosque? What are the competences of the murshidat? Are there any explicit prohibitions on female religious scholars in the Qu'ran or the hadiths?

R. N. M.: Female teachers of religion at all three levels may teach a mixed public in the mosque. When murshidat preside the public tends to be female, particularly because intimate questions concerning marriage and sexual life are dealt with. In such discussion groups the murshidat also fulfil the role of social workers. The alimat, i.e. female religious teachers at the highest level, may address a mixed public on religious topics in a mosque.

In my opinion – and this is in principle the view of Islamic teaching – there are neither verses in the Qu'ran nor hadiths that prohibit a woman from presiding at communal prayer in the mosque. Indeed, one hadith recounts the following story: a woman goes to the prophet and reports that all men are away from the village, the prayer leader is also absent. The prophet instructs her to lead the worship services, in other words to preside at prayer in the mosque.

De facto, though, women never preside at prayers in the mosque. They are hindered by customs and social conventions. The Islamic prayer ritual includes gestures and poses that women prefer not to make in the presence of men. They are embarrassed by it. But this is purely a question of mores.

Although Islam does not prescribe specific places for women in the mosque, women themselves insist on gender separation at prayer. They completely mark off their space with screens and coverings and want to keep to themselves during prayer. They also use a separate entrance to the mosque. Thus, this gender separation is the result of prevailing opinions, moral attitudes and customs.

4) Question: Is it possible to use *ijtihad* (exegesis) to interpret the Qu'ran and the hadiths in a modern way that will allow these sources to provide answers about the equality of women in the twenty-first century?

R. N. M.: The Qu'ran and the hadiths always upheld equality between the genders. Therefore, there is in principle no interpretation. Many Qu'ranic verses confirm this equality. In the hadiths, too, the same duties, but also the same rights, apply to women as to men. Regrettably, with time social customs have overlaid these clear rules about equality. Thus, the impression gradually took hold that it was Islamic law itself that established gender prohibitions or prescribed gender separation. As a result, traditions, morals and customs were mixed with the clear wording of the Qu'ranic verses, and in such a way that in the end the superimpositions were regarded as sacrosanct. In time, the repute of these impositions exceeded to some extent that of the original Qu'ranic text. The traditional teaching about interpretation also encouraged this development. Earlier Islamic scholars let themselves be influenced by social developments, with the result that they often dealt only with religious views that had been overlaid with social traditions and not the pure wording of the Qu'ran. Thus, instead of clarifying this confusion between social conventions and original Qu'ranic text, the superimpositions received an air of official approval and were communicated to the faithful in this form.

It is the task of modern Islamic scholars to again familiarise people with the original texts and to publicise them in their original wording, freed from the layers of social conventions and customs. Female religious scholars in particular must make women aware of their Qu'ranic equality. The enormous problem of illiteracy and ignorance is one reason why this mixture of conventions and original Qu'ranic text is perpetuated. Added to this, it takes courage on the part of women to exercise their rights and, if need be, break (social) taboos.

5) Question: Morocco has a gender-equality provision in its constitution (Art. 19) and has ratified the UN Convention on the Elimination of All Forms of Discrimination against Women. Do such constitutional provisions play a role in the sphere of religion?

R. N. M.: Given that there is no gender discrimination in the Qu'ran, in principle there is no contradiction with international gender-equality law. That said, there is de facto inequality. There is a lack of women leaders both in religion and in politics or who have their hands on other important levers. Women do not demand these positions often or insistently enough.

In our society women still give priority to family and home. Medicine is an interesting phenomenon. The hospitals are now feminised, i.e., there are more female than male doctors. However, medical research comes off badly because, outside of their practical work in the hospital, women are absorbed by their family duties.

6) Question: The inferior status of women in leading spiritual offices contradicts human rights. There is a conflict between traditional practice and women's

rights to equality. One could come to the conclusion that the principle of equality carries greater weight than a long-standing religious tradition that men saw and see as the ideal situation. In general, do you consider a legal solution to the issue of women's rights in religious communities appropriate? Do you think that state law should play a role in filling leading religious offices?

R. N. M.: The growing presence of women will bring change. In the meantime we have feminisation not only in the medical and law faculties, but also in Islamic studies. But it takes time. For centuries women were out of sight; they are now advancing slowly, but gradually. As their presence grows they will increasingly be noticed, or they can make themselves noticed. However, women will have to overcome their phobia about appearing in public.

I do not believe that can be regulated by law. The fact of the presence of women must bring about change. I am not convinced by quota systems. I dislike the message they send: women cannot do it on their own but need the support of quota systems.

Religion is still ubiquitous in our society, even if sometimes it is more a case of tradition than the strict observance of religious rules. For this reason, the role of women in religion will become even more important. Female religious teachers have a gift – whether by nature or socialisation I cannot say – of gently correcting mindsets; and they have an intuitive feeling for women without an educational background and are able to familiarise them with the actual contents of the Qu'ran. This in turn helps reduce a social tendency to fanaticism and violence. For, as a rule, people who exhibit such fanatical tendencies do not know their Qu'ran very well.

7) Question: Morocco is taking a pragmatic approach by opening up Islamic education to women. This solution depends on the goodwill of the (male) authorities. If practice continues to discriminate on the basis of gender, what other enforcement possibilities do Muslim women have?

R. N. M.: We are moving in a direction that can no longer be reversed. The training for the murshidat is now institutionally organised. Therefore, we may predict that in the future the situation will change only for the better, not for the worse. To take advantage of these opportunities women now have to make an effort. The engine is there and it is running. Thus, in future there will be more female teachers of religion at all levels. This increased female presence will change the landscape – I am convinced of this. One can already feel that, with the increase in the number of female students in all disciplines, something is changing at the universities. In my day (1997) it was still possible to be the first Moroccan woman to obtain a doctorate in constitutional law.

Rajaa Naji al Makkawi, PhD, lives in Rabat with her husband and four adult children. The interview (in French) with the law professor and Islam expert took place there on 3 June 2013.

Glossary

Ramadan Lectures	Solemn series of lectures in the month of Ramadan, presided over by King Mohammed VI and attended by leading representatives of political, diplomatic and academic circles and by ulama from around the world; for centuries prior to 2003 the lectures had been reserved exclusively to male Islamic scholars
Qu'ran	Revealed scripture of Islam; it consists of 114 suras
Hadiths	Contain the sayings, rulings and actions of the Prophet Mohammed collected by his companions and the following generations[194]
Ijtihad	Refers to the efforts to interpret the Qu'ran and hadiths to arrive at legal rulings; since the tenth century Muslim scholars have been demanding the "closing of the gate of ijtihad" as authoritative interpretations of all religious texts already exist; reformists see interpretation as a way of adapting the law to reflect contemporary developments[195]
Fatwa	Legal opinion that provides an answer to a specific issue pertaining to Islamic law[196]

Three levels of Islamic scholarship

1) ulama/alimat	Highest level of academic training; most ulama and alimat, their female equivalents, work as university professors
2) Second level	Islamic studies, possibly a doctorate, but knowledge and reputation less far-reaching than the first level
3) imam/murshidat	Training in pastoral care without scientific specialisation; 2003: creation of a training institute for imams and murshidat in Rabat; prerequisite for admission is a university degree

---

[194] See *Elger*, pp. 118 ff. (Hadîth).

[195] See *Elger*, p. 135 (Ijtihâd).

[196] See *Elger*, p. 101 (Fatwâ).

Bibliography

Ahlers, Stella, Gleichstellung der Frau in Staat und Kirche – ein problematisches Spannungsverhältnis, Münster 2006

Amirpur, Katajun, Den Islam neu denken, Der Dschihad für Demokratie, Freiheit und Frauenrechte, Munich 2013

Arx, Urs von, Die Debatte über die Frauenordination in den Altkatholischen Kirchen der Utrechter Union, in: Denise Buser/Adrian Loretan (eds), Gleichstellung der Geschlechter und die Kirchen, Ein Beitrag zur menschenrechtlichen und ökumenischen Diskussion, Fribourg 1999, pp. 165 ff.

Bausenhart, Guido, Das Amt in der Kirche, Eine notwendende Neubestimmung, Freiburg/Basel/Vienna 1999

Bayes, Jane H./Tohidi, Nayereh (eds), Globalization, Gender and Religion, The Politics of Women's Rights in Catholic and Muslim Contexts, Basingstoke 2001

Beinert, Wolfgang, Dogmatische Überlegungen zum Thema Priestertum der Frau, in: Walter Gross (ed.), Frauenordination, Stand der Diskussion in der Katholischen Kirche, Munich 1996, pp. 64 ff.

Bernhardt, Reinhold/Kuhn, Thomas K. (eds), Religionsfreiheit, Schweizerische Perspektiven, Zurich 2007

Biaggini, Giovanni/Gächter, Thomas/Kiener, Regina (eds), Staatsrecht, 2nd ed., Zurich/St. Gallen 2015

Bigler-Eggenberger, Margrith, Die schweizerische Bundesverfassung, St. Galler Kommentar, 2nd ed., Zurich/St. Gallen 2008, Article 8

Bigler-Eggenberger, Margrith/Kägi-Diener, Regula, Die schweizerische Bundesverfassung, St. Galler Kommentar, 3rd ed., Zurich/St. Gallen 2014, Article 8

Brodbeck, Doris (ed.), Unerhörte Worte, Religiöse Gesellschaftskritik von Frauen im 20. Jahrhundert, Berne/Wettingen 2003

Brodbeck, Doris/Domhardt, Yvonne/Stofer, Judith (eds), Siehe, ich schaffe Neues, Aufbrüche von Frauen in Protestantismus, Katholizismus, Christkatholizismus und Judentum, Berne 1998

Brosi, Urs, Recht, Strukturen, Freiräume, Zurich 2013

Büchler, Andrea, Religiöse und kulturelle Identität und Gleichstellung der Geschlechter insbesondere im familienrechtlichen Kontext. Oder: Islamisches Recht in der Schweiz?, in: René Pahud de Mortanges (ed.), Religion und Integration aus der Sicht des Rechts, Grundlagen – Problemfelder – Perspektiven, Zurich/Basel/Geneva 2010, pp. 81 ff.

Buser, Denise/Loretan, Adrian (eds), Gleichstellung der Geschlechter und die Kirchen, Ein Beitrag zur menschenrechtlichen und ökumenischen Diskussion, Fribourg 1999

Buser, Denise, Die katholische Priesterin – ein (juristisches) Hirngespinst?, in: Monika Egger/Livia Meier/Katja Wissmiller (eds), WoMan in Church, Kirche und Amt im Kontext der Geschlechterfrage, Berlin 2006, pp. 53 ff.

Campenhausen, Axel von/de Wall, Heinrich, Staatskirchenrecht, Eine systematische Darstellung des Religionsverfassungsrechts in Deutschland und Europa, 4th ed., Munich 2006

Daly, Mary, Jenseits von Gottvater Sohn & Co., Aufbruch zu einer Philosophie der Frauenbefreiung, 5th ed., Munich 1988

Demel, Sabine, Frauen und kirchliches Amt, Vom Ende eines Tabus in der katholischen Kirche, Freiburg/Basel/Vienna 2004, followed by an updated version: Frauen und kirchliches Amt, Grundlagen – Grenzen – Möglichkeiten, Freiburg/Basel/Vienna 2012 (quoted as "2012")

Egger, Monika/Meier, Livia/Wissmiller, Katja (eds), WoMan in Church, Kirche und Amt im Kontext der Geschlechterfrage, Berlin 2006

Elger, Ralf (ed.), Kleines Islam-Lexikon, Geschichte Alltag Kultur, 5th ed., Munich 2008

Eidgenössische Kommission für Frauenfragen, Gleichstellung der Geschlechter und kulturelle/religiöse Praktiken, in: Frauenfragen/Questions au féminin/Questioni femminili, Schwerpunkt: Frauenrechte – Kultur – Religion 1/2 2010, pp. 12 ff.

Eisen, Ute E., Amtsträgerinnen im frühen Christentum, Epigraphische und literarische Studien, Göttingen 1996

Felber, Anneliese, Lehren oder Kinderkriegen? 1 Tim. 2 in der patristischen Rezeption, in: Fischer, Irmtraud/Heil, Christoph (eds), Geschlechterverhältnisse und Macht, Lebensformen in der Zeit des frühen Christentums, Vienna 2010, pp. 197 ff.

Fischer, Irmtraud/Heil, Christoph (eds), Geschlechterverhältnisse und Macht, Lebensformen in der Zeit des frühen Christentums, Vienna 2010

Freeman, Marsha A. et al. (eds), The UN Convention on the Elimination of All Forms of Discrimination against Women, Oxford 2012

Freivogel, Elisabeth, Art. 3 Diskriminierungsverbot, in: Claudia Kaufmann (ed.), Kommentar zum Gleichstellungsgesetz, 2nd ed., Basel 2009, pp. 48 ff.

Frerk, Carsten, Violettbuch Kirchenfinanzen, Wie der Staat die Kirchen finanziert, Aschaffenburg 2010

Greenspahn, Frederick E. (ed.), Women and Judaism, New Insights and Scholarship, New York/London 2009

Gross, Walter (ed.), Frauenordination, Stand der Diskussion in der Katholischen Kirche, Munich 1996 (quoted as "Frauenordination")

Gross, Walter, Bericht der Päpstlichen Bibelkommission, 1976, in: Walter Gross (ed.), Frauenordination, Stand der Diskussion in der Katholischen Kirche, Munich 1996, pp. 25 ff. (quoted as "Bericht")

Gössmann, Elisabeth et al. (eds), Wörterbuch der Feministischen Theologie, Gütersloh 2002

Häfelin, Ulrich/Müller, Georg/Uhlman, Felix, Allgemeines Verwaltungsrecht, 7th ed., Zurich/St. Gallen 2016

Häfelin, Ulrich/Haller, Walter/Keller, Helen/Thurnherr Daniela, Schweizerisches Bundesstaatsrecht, 9th ed., Zurich/Basel/Geneva 2016

Hafner, Felix, Religionsfreiheit im Kontext der Menschenrechte, in: Adrian Loretan (ed.), Religionsfreiheit im Kontext der Grundrechte, Religionsrechtliche Studien, vol. 2, Zurich 2011, pp. 121 ff. (quoted as "Religionsfreiheit")

Hafner, Felix, Kirche und Demokratie, Betrachtungen aus juristischer Sicht, in: Schweizerisches Jahrbuch für Kirchenrecht, 1997, vol. 2, pp. 37 ff. (quoted as "Demokratie")

Hafner, Felix, Trennung von Kirche und Staat, Anspruch und Wirklichkeit, in: Basler Juristische Mitteilungen, bulletin 5/1996, pp. 225 ff. (quoted as "Trennung")

Hafner, Felix, Staatskirchenrecht im Spannungsfeld von Kirche und Politik, in: Adrian Loretan (ed.), Kirche – Staat im Umbruch, Neuere Entwicklungen im Verhältnis von Kirchen und anderen Religionsgemeinschaften, Zurich 1995, pp. 33 ff. (quoted as "Spannungsfeld")

Hafner, Felix, Kirchen im Kontext der Grund- und Menschenrechte, Fribourg 1992 (quoted as "Kirchen")

Hafner, Felix/Brosi, Urs, Bischöfliche Personalentscheide und landeskirchliches Recht, Basel 2007

Hafner, Felix/Buser, Denise, Frauenordination via Gleichstellungsgesetz? Die Anwendbarkeit des Gleichstellungsgesetzes auf die Dienstverhältnisse in der römisch-katholischen Kirche, in: Aktuelle Juristische Praxis 1996, pp. 1207 ff.

Hallensleben, Barbara, Freiburger Zeitschrift für Philosophie und Theologie, 47 (2000), pp. 288 ff.

Hainz Mc Grath, Elsie/Meehan, Bridget Mary/Raming, Ida, Frauen finden einen Weg: die internationale Bewegung römisch-katholische Priesterinnen, Berlin 2009

Hauke, Manfred, Die Problematik um das Frauenpriestertum vor dem Hintergrund der Schöpfungs- und Erlösungsordnung, Paderborn 1995

Heinzelmann, Gertrud, Die geheiligte Diskriminierung: Beiträge zum kirchlichen Feminismus, Bonstetten 1986

Hesse, Konrad, Grundzüge des Verfassungsrechts der Bundesrepublik Deutschland, 20th ed., Heidelberg 1995

Huber, Wolfgang, Gerechtigkeit und Recht, Grundlinien christlicher Rechtsethik, Gütersloh 1996

Hünermann, Peter, Schwerwiegende Bedenken. Eine Analyse des Apostolischen Schreibens "Ordinatio Sacerdotalis", in: Walter Gross (ed.), Frauenordination, Stand der Diskussion in der Katholischen Kirche, Munich 1996, pp. 120 ff.

Isensee, Josef, Das Grundrecht als Abwehrrecht und als staatliche Schutzpflicht, in: Josef Isensee/Paul Kirchhof (eds), Handbuch des Staatsrechts der Bundesrepublik Deutschland, 3rd ed., Heidelberg 2011

Jensen, Anne, Frauenordination und ökumenischer Dialog, in: Walter Gross (ed.), Frauenordination, Stand der Diskussion in der Katholischen Kirche, Munich 1996, pp. 100 ff.

Jones, Ian et al. (eds), Women and Ordination in the Christian Churches, International Perspectives, London 2008

Kirchschläger, Peter G., Wie können Menschenrechte begründet werden? Ein für religiöse und säkulare Menschenrechtskonzeptionen anschlussfähiger Ansatz, Münster 2013

Kley, Andreas, Geschichte des öffentlichen Rechts der Schweiz, Zurich/St. Gallen 2011

Kopp, Barbara, Die Unbeirrbare, Wie Gertrud Heinzelmann den Papst und die Schweiz das Fürchten lehrte, Zurich 2003

Kraus, Dieter, Religionsfreiheit im europäischen Recht, in: Adrian Loretan (ed.), Religionsfreiheit im Kontext der Grundrechte, Religionsrechtliche Studien, vol. 2, Zurich 2011, pp. 189 ff. (quoted as "Religionsfreiheit")

Kraus, Dieter, Schweizerisches Staatskirchenrecht, Tübingen 1993 (quoted as "Staatskirchenrecht")

Kröni, Tanja, Männliche Scheidungsverweigerung im Judentum und ihre Folgen, in: Judith Stofer/Rifa'at Lenzin (eds), Körperlichkeit, Ein interreligiös-feministischer Dialog, Markt Zell 2007, pp. 127 ff.

Laurien, Hanna-Renate, Abgeschrieben? Plädoyer für eine faire Diskussion über das Priestertum der Frau, Basel 1995

Loretan, Adrian, Religionen im Kontext der Menschenrechte, Religionsrechtliche Studien, vol. 1, Zurich 2010 (quoted as "Volume 1")

Loretan, Adrian (ed.), Religionsfreiheit im Kontext der Grundrechte, Religionsrechtliche Studien, vol. 2, Zurich 2011 (quoted as "Volume 2")

Loretan, Adrian, Frauen in kirchlichen Ämtern. Eine rechtliche Standortbestimmung, in: Denise Buser/Adrian Loretan (eds), Gleichstellung der Geschlechter und die Kirchen, Ein Beitrag zur menschenrechtlichen und ökumenischen Diskussion, Fribourg 1999, pp. 52 ff. (quoted as "Frauen")

Loretan, Adrian (ed.), Kirche – Staat im Umbruch, Neuere Entwicklungen im Verhältnis von Kirchen und anderen Religionsgemeinschaften, Zurich 1995

Kokott, Juliane/Mager, Ute (eds), Religionsfreiheit und Gleichberechtigung der Geschlechter, Spannungen und ungelöste Konflikte, Tübingen 2014

Macy, Gary, The Hidden History of Women's Ordination, Female Clergy in the Medieval West, New York 2008

Manea, Elham, Ich will nicht mehr schweigen, Der Islam, der Westen und die Menschenrechte, Freiburg i. Br. 2010

Martin, Céline, Grundrechtskollisionen, Basel 2007

Mieth, Dietmar, Haben Frauen ein Recht auf das Priestertum? in: Walter Gross (ed.), Frauenordination, Stand der Diskussion in der Katholischen Kirche, Munich 1996, pp. 97 ff.

Moltmann-Wendel, Elisabeth, Frauen um Jesus, Gütersloh 2009

Müller, Gerhard Ludwig (ed.), Frauen in der Kirche, Eigensein und Mitverantwortung, Würzburg 1999

Müller, Gerhard Ludwig, Kann nur der getaufte Mann gültig das Weihesakrament empfangen? Zur Lehrentscheidung in "Ordinatio Sacerdotalis", in: Müller, Gerhard Ludwig (ed.), Frauen in der Kirche, Eigensein und Mitverantwortung, Würzburg 1999, pp. 278 ff. (quoted as "Weihesakrament")

Müller, Iris/Raming, Ida, Unser Leben im Einsatz für Menschenrechte der Frauen in der römisch-katholischen Kirche: Lebensberichte – Hintergründe – Dokumente – Ausblick, Berlin 2007

Nagl-Docekal, Herta, Geschlechtergerechtigkeit: Wie könnte eine philosophische Perspektive für die theologische Debatte von Relevanz sein?, in: Theologische Quartalschrift 195 (2015), pp. 74 ff.

Nadell, Pamela S., Women and American Judaism, in: Frederick E. Greenspahn (ed.), Women and Judaism, New York/London 2009, pp. 155 ff.

Pemsel-Maier, Sabine (ed.), Zwischen Alltag und Ausnahme: Seelsorgerinnen, Geschichte, Theologie und gegenwärtige Praxis, Ostfildern 2001

Raming, Ida/Müller, Iris, "Contra legem" – a Matter of Conscience, Our Lifelong Struggle for Human Rights for Women in the Roman-Catholic Church, Berlin 2010 (quoted as "contra legem")

Raming, Ida, Gleichrangig in Christus anstatt: Ausschluss von Frauen "im Namen Gottes", Zur Rezeption und Interpretation von Gal. 3,27 f in vatikanischen Dokumenten, Berlin 2006 (quoted as "Gleichrangig")

Raming, Ida, Priesteramt der Frau – Geschenk Gottes für eine erneuerte Kirche, Münster 2002 (quoted as "Priesteramt")

Raming, Ida et al. (eds), Zur Priesterin berufen: Gott sieht nicht auf das Geschlecht, Zeugnisse römisch-katholischer Frauen, Thaur/Vienna/Munich 1998

Raming, Ida, Der Ausschluss der Frau vom priesterlichen Amt: gottgewollte Tradition oder Diskriminierung? Eine rechtshistorisch-dogmatische Untersuchung der Grundlagen von Kanon 968 § 1 des Codex Iuris Canonici, Köln 1973

Ranke-Heinemann, Uta, Eunuchen für das Himmelreich, Katholische Kirche und Sexualität, 2nd ed., Hamburg 1988

Ratzinger, Joseph, Das Priestertum des Mannes – ein Verstoss gegen die Rechte der Frau?, in: Gerhard Ludwig Müller (ed.), Frauen in der Kirche, Eigensein und Mitverantwortung, Würzburg 1999, pp. 267 ff.

Reininger, Dorothea, Diakonat der Frau in der Einen Kirche, Diskussionen, Entscheidungen und pastoral-praktische Erfahrungen in der christlichen Ökumene und ihr Beitrag zur römisch-katholischen Diskussion, Ostfildern 1999

Rhinow, René/Schefer, Markus/Uebersax Peter, Schweizerisches Verfassungsrecht, 3rd ed., Basel 2016

Reuter, Astrid/Kippenberg, Hans G., Religionskonflikte im Verfassungsstaat, Göttingen 2010

Sahlfeld, Konrad, Die Religionsfreiheit in der Schweiz, Grundlage für eine Debatte zur religiösen Öffnung der Schweiz, in: Reinhold Bernhardt/Thomas K. Kuhn (eds), Religionsfreiheit, Schweizerische Perspektiven, Zurich 2007, pp. 71 ff.

Schefer, Markus, Die Beeinträchtigung von Grundrechten, Zur Dogmatik von Art. 36 BV, Berne 2006

Schüngel-Straumann, Helen, Anfänge feministischer Exegese, Münster 2002, reprint Münster 2013 (quoted as "Anfänge")

Schüngel-Straumann, Helen, Eva, Die erste Frau der Bibel: Ursache allen Übels? Paderborn 2014 (quoted as "Eva")

Schüssler Fiorenza, Elisabeth, Grenzen überschreiten: der theoretische Anspruch feministischer Theologie, Münster 2004

Sepp, Peter, Geheime Weihen, Die Frauen in der verborgenen tschechoslowakischen Kirche Koinótes, Ostfildern 2004

Spenlé, Christoph A./Mugier, Simon, Geschichte der Menschenrechte: Entwicklungen im Spannungsfeld von Individuum und Kollektiv, in: Adrian Loretan (ed.), Religionsfreiheit im Kontext der Grundrechte, Religionsrechtliche Studien, vol. 2, Zurich 2011, pp. 43 ff.

Spielmann, Christoph, Konkurrenz von Grundrechtsnormen, Baden-Baden 2008

Stofer, Judith, "Den Sexismus endlich überwinden", in: Judith Stofer/Rifa'at Lenzin (eds), Körperlichkeit, Ein interreligiös-feministischer Dialog, Markt Zell 2007, pp. 169 ff.

Strahm, Doris/Rudolf, Heidi, Leitungsfunktionen von Frauen im Christentum, in: Doris Strahm (ed.), Rabbinerinnen, Kantorinnen, Imaminnen, Muftis, Pfarrerinnen, Bischöfinnen, Kirchenrätinnen, Leitungsfunktionen von Frauen im Judentum, im Christentum und im Islam, Basel 2011, pp. 31 ff.

Strahm, Doris (ed.), Rabbinerinnen, Kantorinnen, Imaminnen, Muftis, Pfarrerinnen, Bischöfinnen, Kirchenrätinnen, Leitungsfunktionen von Frauen im Judentum, im Christentum und im Islam, Basel 2011 (online publication 2011: http://www.interrelthinktank.ch/, last downloaded June 2015)

Sullivan, Donna J., Gender Equality and Religious Freedom: Toward a Framework for Conflict Resolution, in: International Law and Politics, vol. 24 (1992), pp. 795 ff.

Sunstein, Cass R., On the Tension between Sex Equality and Religious Freedom, in: Silvio Ferrari/Rinaldo Cristofori (eds), The Library of essays on law and religion, vol. 4: Current Issues in Law and Religion, Surrey 2013, pp. 367 ff.

Swidler, Leonard/Swidler, Arlene (eds), Women priests, A Catholic Commentary on the Vatican Declaration, New York/Ramsey/Toronto 1977

Taschl-Erber, Andrea, "Eva wird Apostel!", Rezeptionslinien des Osterapostolats Marias von Magdala in der lateinischen Patristik, in: Irmtraud Fischer/Christoph Heil (eds), Geschlechterverhältnisse und Macht, Lebensformen in der Zeit des frühen Christentums, Vienna 2010, pp. 161 ff.

Theologische Realenzyklopädie, Berlin 2009 ff. (online version)

Traitler, Reinhild, Leitungsfunktionen von Frauen in den Kirchen der Reformation, in: Doris Strahm (ed.), Rabbinerinnen, Kantorinnen, Imaminnen, Muftis, Pfarrerinnen, Bischöfinnen, Kirchenrätinnen, Leitungsfunktionen von Frauen im Judentum, im Christentum und im Islam, Basel 2011, pp. 47 ff.

Unruh, Peter, Zur Dogmatik der grundrechtlichen Schutzpflichten, Berlin 1996

Wallach-Faller, Marianne, Die Frau im Tallit, Judentum feministisch gelesen, Zurich 2000

Wijngaards, John, The Ordination of Women in the Catholic Church, Unmasking a Cuckoo's Egg Tradition, Delhi 2002

Wyler, Bea, Welche Gemeinde antwortet auf mein Qaddisch?, in: Doris Brodbeck/Yvonne Domhardt/Judith Stofer (eds), Siehe, ich schaffe Neues, Aufbrüche von Frauen in Protestantismus, Katholizismus, Christkatholizismus und Judentum, Berne 1998, pp. 229 ff.

Wyttenbach, Judith, Kooperation von Staat und Religionsgemeinschaften in der Schweiz im Kontext der Grundrechte, in: Adrian Loretan (ed.), Religionsfreiheit im Kontext der Grundrechte, Religionsrechtliche Studien, vol. 2, Zurich 2011, pp. 377 ff.

Wolgast, Eike, Geschichte der Menschen- und Bürgerrechte, Stuttgart 2009

Abbreviations

Art.	Article
AGG	Equal Treatment Act (Allgemeines Gleichbehandlungsgesetz)
can./cann.	canon/canones; provisions of the CIC
CE	Common or Current Era
CEDAW	Convention on the Elimination of All Forms of Discrimination against Women of 18 December 1979 (SR 0.108)
CIC	Codex Iuris Canonici, Code of canon law of 1983
DAZ	successor journal (1992-1997) to "Volksrecht"
EC	European Community (today: EU, European Union)
ed./eds	editor/edition/editors
EEC	European Economic Community (today: EU, European Union)
ECHR	European Convention for the Protection of Human Rights and Fundamental Freedoms
et al.	et allii/aliae (and others)
EU	European Union
f./ff.	and the following page/pages, paragraphs etc.
fn.	footnote
FSC	Swiss Federal Supreme Court
Gal.	Galatians, Epistle from Paul to the Galatians
ibid.	ibidem (in the same place)
ILO	International Labour Organization
KiV	Constitution of the Roman Catholic Regional Church of the Canton Basel-Landschaft of 10 February 1976
mn.	margin number
n.	note
no.	number
para.	paragraph
p./pp.	page/pages

SFC	Federal Constitution of the Swiss Confederation of 18 April 1999 (SR 101)
SG	classified compilations of legislation (of the Swiss Cantons)
SR	classified compilation of the legislation of the Swiss Confederation
TFEU	Treaty on the Functioning of the European Union of 25 March 1957 (as amended)
UN Covenant I	International Covenant of 16 December 1966 on Economic, Social and Cultural Rights (SR 0.103.1)
UN Covenant II	International Covenant of 16 December 1966 on Civil and Political Rights (SR 0.103.2)
vol.	volume

Photo credits

Dr Ida Raming, Asemwald/Stuttgart, December 2012
Rabbi Bea Wyler, Basel, April 2013
Rajaa Naji al Makkawi, PhD, Rabat (Morocco), June 2013
Photos: D. Buser